Praise for *The First Spiritual Exercises: Four Guided Retreats*

"A beautiful book and an important one as well. Michael Hansen, S.J., an experienced Jesuit retreat director and a talented writer, recovers an often-overlooked way of praying with St. Ignatius Loyola's Spiritual Exercises. But this is much more than a guide for a fulfilling personal retreat; it is also a compendium of inspiring meditations, useful insights, and practical advice for anyone who seeks a closer relationship with God. In these pages is a wealth of knowledge that I will surely be using in the future—both in counseling others and in my own prayer life."

James Martin, S.J.
Author of *The Jesuit Guide to (Almost) Everything*

"*The First Spiritual Exercises*, written and piloted by Fr. Michael Hansen, S.J., is an important breakthrough in our understanding of the Spiritual Exercises and for potentially extending an experience of the Spiritual Exercises of St. Ignatius to many, many more people of all ages than other more familiar forms of the Exercises. The author's impeccable research briefly opens a window onto Ignatius's earliest practices in giving this first version of the Exercises and invites the reader to experience one or more of these four-week experiences for oneself. His prose is both attractive and enlightening. Each one of the retreats highlights essential aspects of the Ignatian vision of a God who desires to grace each retreatant with a relationship of mutuality and friendship in the service of others and the Gospel. Great care is displayed in the inclusion of texts for and about women as well as grounding every retreat in key Gospel texts that introduce the person making these Exercises to a deeply Gospel spirituality as well as Ignatian approaches to prayer and transformation into discipleship."

Janet K. Ruffing, R.S.M.
Professor in the Practice of Spirituality and Ministerial Leadership
Yale Divinity School

"Michael Hansen, S.J., helps readers meet the living God who wants a personal relationship with them. From years of experience he knows the Spiritual Exercises of St. Ignatius of Loyola very well and leads the reader in a creative and easy-to-follow way through them without jargon and with a deft hand. I am very happy to recommend this book and I sense that St. Ignatius rejoices that his great work has been made so accessible to modern readers."

William A. Barry, S.J.
Author of *A Friendship Like No Other*

"Prayer is better learned by doing it, although there are many good books about prayer. Michael Hansen, S.J., lures us to pray in his recent book, *The First Spiritual Exercises*. Though the book is professionally footnoted with the Spiritual Exercises of St. Ignatius Loyola, this master artisan entices us into such a simple method of prayer that soon we feel as though we have been praying this all our life."

George Aschenbrenner, S.J.
Author of *Stretched for Greater Glory: The Spiritual Exercises*

"If you are looking for a clear, simple, and practical approach to developing your prayer life in the Ignatian tradition, *The First Spiritual Exercises* is well worth procuring. One of Ignatius's most radical and contentious insights was that the Creator engages directly with the heart of the creature. What I particularly like about the exercises in *The First Spiritual Exercises* is that they invite, stimulate, and give us freedom, if we dare, to dispose ourselves to experience such an encounter."

Brendan Kelly, S.J.
Master of Jesuit Novices
Australia

"These are challenging times for Christians trying to sustain a lively faith. Growing disillusionment with institutional religion and turbulent controversies within mainline denominations pose serious hurdles in our walk of faith. These present conditions parallel the historical situation in which Ignatius of Loyola introduced his Spiritual Exercises as a practical way of grounding faith in concrete personal experience of God's love, forgiveness, call, and faithfulness in one's life. Jesuit Michael Hansen's *The First Spiritual Exercises* captures in a helpful way Ignatius's process of spiritual renewal and makes it an accessible and useful tool for deepening an intimate connection with God today. I highly recommend it."

Wilkie Au
Professor of Theological Studies
Loyola Marymount University

"Michael Hansen has graced us with a fresh look at Saint Ignatius's Spiritual Exercises. Rooted deep in both Ignatius's understanding of the spiritual life and also the realities of Christian discipleship in the contemporary world, Hansen offers us a thorough immersion in the Ignatian school of divine love. I highly recommend Hansen's text for use among religious and lay people, in retreat centers, in schools, in parishes, and in conversations among friends. He extends to us Ignatius's conviction that God deals directly with his beloved creatures and invites us to deepen our response to God's generous love."

Tim Muldoon
Author of *The Ignatian Workout*

"This work is astoundingly clear, faithful to the Spiritual Exercises, and beautiful as well."

Marlene Marburg
Campion Centre of Ignatian Spirituality
Melbourne, Australia

"This is one of the great books on Ignatian Spirituality. It takes people from where Ignatius first found them, in their prayers and devotions, and quickly moves them into formal prayer. I have been using it for four years, and those to whom I have given it marvel at its power to move them into an intimate relationship with God. Michael Hansen is a born teacher who enables people through the use of imagination to experience and reflect on their experience of God's love and discover its dynamic in their own selves."

Des Purcell, S.J.
Director of Canisius Centre of Ignatian Spirituality
Sydney, Australia

the FIRST
Spiritual
EXERCISES

A Manual for Those Who Give the Exercises

Michael Hansen, S.J.

ave maria press AmP notre dame, indiana

Founded in 1865, Ave Maria Press is a ministry of the United States Province of Holy Cross.

www.avemariapress.com

Paperback: ISBN-10 1-59471-380-4, ISBN-13 978-1-59471-380-4

E-book: ISBN-10 1-59471-381-2, ISBN-13 978-1-59471-381-1

Cover image © CORBIS.

Cover and text design by David Scholtes.

Printed and bound in the United States of America.

Library of Congress Cataloging-in-Publication Data

Dedicated
to the first companions of Ignatius,
the original givers of the First Spiritual Exercises;
to the lay givers of the First Spiritual Exercises
from the time of the first companions until now;
to Christian Life Community
on their 450th anniversary
of living the First Spiritual Exercises;
and to the Campion CIS Outreach Team,
the first modern givers
of this First Spiritual Exercises.

The Spiritual Exercises

is the very best thing that in this life,

I can think, perceive or understand

for helping a person benefit himself

as well as bringing fruit, benefit, and advantage to many others;

for even if you felt no need for the former,

you will see immeasurably and incomparably

you will be helped with regard to the latter.

—Ignatius, Letter 10

You received without payment; give without payment

—Matthew 10:8–9

Take Lord and receive,

all my liberty, my memory, my understanding

and my entire will, all that I have and possess.

You gave it all to me; to you I return it.

All is yours, dispose of it entirely according to your will.

Give me only your love and your grace,

that is enough for me.

—*Spiritual Exercises* 231–35

CONTENTS

INTRODUCTION

___

"Give, and it will be given to you. A good measure, pressed down, shaken together, running over, will be put into your lap" (Lk 6:38). You have received the First Spiritual Exercises (FSE) and its overflowing graces, and you desire to share it with others. The purpose of this Manual is to encourage, help, and support you in this desire. With it, you can better direct the flow of gifts from the FSE.

In this work, you have three identities and roles: Friend of God, which you are already, and Spiritual Conversation Guide and Giver of the FSE, which you may desire to become. These roles are represented in the structure of the Manual, training you for each one of these identities.

The FSE is all about receiving and giving. In the language of the prayer that serves as the epigraph of this Manual, Ignatius speaks of receiving and giving. "Take Lord and receive, all my liberty, my memory, my understanding and my entire will, all that I have and possess. You gave it all to me; to you I return it." This is the language that will be used in this Manual. You are the "giver" of the FSE. The person making the retreat is the "receiver." In the FSE there are actually four lives that receive and give together: Jesus, Ignatius, you, and your receiver.

Echoing the words of Jesus (Jn 13:20), whoever receives you receives the First Spiritual Exercises, and whoever receives the First Spiritual Exercises receives Jesus and the one who sent him.

From the beginning Ignatius intended the FSE to serve three needs:

1. to give the receiver the desired retreat,

2. to provide the receiver with exercises to use after the retreat,

3. to teach your receiver how to instruct others in these exercises.

This is the ripple effect of the FSE. Each receiver becomes a giver in some manner. And many people, like yourself, spread out into the community, giving the FSE retreats across all sorts of boundaries and renewing lives. This is the dream and energy of the FSE.

1

Here are three things that may free you from any initial anxiety:

1. All you need do is give the exercise. Your receiver pours her or his life into it.

2. The effect of the FSE is with God and your receiver. It is not in your hands.

3. You will not be alone. You have the Spirit and a partner as cogivers, and if possible a mentor for your first retreats.

Your own experience of receiving the FSE is your best teacher in giving the FSE. Actually giving these retreats to others is the next best teacher. So this Manual is the teacher that sits between these two. You need all three. The Manual teaches an exercise or process through commentary. To keep step with your receiver, it will, at times, closely replicate the text in the book *The First Spiritual Exercises*.

Though Catholic in origin, the FSE is inclusive of all Christian traditions, searchers, and unchurched. It is for all people—the disadvantaged, youth, workers, professionals, the influential, the middle class, the poor, leaders, parishioners, teachers, prisoners, the sick, the confused, the lost . . . anyone looking for inner peace.

WARNING: Please do not read this Manual before receiving a First Spiritual Exercises retreat. It will create very unhelpful expectations and seriously intrude between God and you in your retreat.

The Spirit of the Lord Is upon You

The time is ripe. "Do you not say, 'Four months more, then comes the harvest'? But I tell you, look around you, and see how the fields are ripe for harvesting" (Jn 4:35). In your hands, the FSE stands ready to help. But before giving you the particular guidance in this Manual, two general helps are offered now.

The first is a "Sending Meditation," a short spiritual exercise that reveals the purpose of the FSE and its way of proceeding. This gospel text was the foundational inspiration for Ignatius and his companions of their own identity and desires. Like you, they wanted to serve this way under Jesus. Of course how you move into communities, through new technologies and presence, and in what ways you apply the FSE with particular people, is as challenging today as it was for the first disciples.

The second is a "Sending Blessing," for every time you find yourself sent out to give an exercise, or a number of them, or a whole FSE retreat. Both the sending meditation and the sending blessing are provided here, before anything else, as places you might return to often during your work with the FSE and find life.

The Sending Meditation

This is a short prayer, seven minutes at most, for when the time is ripe. It is the story of Jesus' desire for me. First I read it in its entirety, then I choose one of the ten parts with its pair of points that attracts me. I close my eyes, enter the scene, and stand before Jesus on the mountain. I take my place with the women and men he has called to send out. He addresses me personally. Then I listen to him and respond with feeling.

1. *The spirit of the Lord God is upon me, because the Lord has anointed me; he has sent me to bring good news to the oppressed, to bind up the brokenhearted, to proclaim liberty to the captives, and release to the prisoners; to proclaim the year of the Lord's favor. . . . To provide for those who mourn in Zion, to give them a garland instead of ashes, the oil of gladness instead of mourning, the mantle of praise instead of a faint spirit* (Is 61:1–3).

    Point 1. Jesus accepts the call to bind broken hearts and liberate. So have you.

    Point 2. The FSE is affirmation, praise, and gladness. It strengthens faint spirits.

2. *When Jesus saw the crowds, he had compassion for them, because they were harassed and helpless, like sheep without a shepherd. Then he said to his disciples, "The harvest is plentiful, but the laborers are few; therefore ask the Lord of the harvest to send out laborers into his harvest"* (Mt 9:36–38).

    Point 1. Jesus feels compassion for the helpless and the lost. So he sends you.

Point 2. The FSE guides, shepherds, and helps those who are harassed.

3. *Jesus went up the mountain and called to him those whom he wanted, and they came to him. And he appointed twelve, whom he also named apostles, to be with him (Mk 3:13–15). Now during those days he went out to the mountain to pray; and he spent the night in prayer to God (Lk 6:12–13).*

Point 1. Jesus called to him those he wanted. He wants you. And you have come.

Point 2. The FSE brings prayer to important choices. It frees people for service.

4. *These twelve Jesus sent out with the following instructions: "As you go, proclaim the good news, 'The kingdom of heaven has come near.' Cure the sick, raise the dead, cleanse the lepers, cast out demons" (Mt 10:1,5,7–8).*

Point 1. Jesus gives his disciples his own mission. He reveals these needs to you.

Point 2. The FSE brings Jesus to the sick, lifeless, rejected, and unfree.

5. *You received without payment; give without payment. Take no gold, silver, or copper in your belts, no bag for your journey, or two tunics, or sandals, or a staff; for laborers deserve their food (Mt 10:9–10).*

Point 1. Jesus is very clear: what was freely received is freely given.

Point 2. The FSE takes no baggage, goes with free hands, and seeks local hospitality.

6. *Whatever town or village you enter, find out who in it is worthy, and stay there until you leave. As you enter the house, greet it. If the house is worthy, let your peace come upon it; but if it is not worthy, let your peace return to you (Mt 10:11–12).*

Point 1. Jesus says find, stay with, and serve those who are ready and open.

Point 2. The FSE is about receiving and giving the deep inner peace of God.

7. *After this the Lord appointed seventy others and sent them on ahead of him in pairs to every town and place where he himself intended to go. "Whoever listens to you listens to me, and whoever rejects you rejects me, and whoever*

rejects me rejects the one who sent me" (Lk 10:1,16).

Point 1. Jesus sent his disciples in pairs. Find yourself a partner.

Point 2. FSE: In listening to you, receivers hear Jesus, and the one who sent him.

8. *The seventy returned with joy, saying, "Lord, in your name even the demons submit to us!" Jesus said to them, "I watched Satan fall from heaven like a flash of lightning. See, I have given you authority to tread on snakes and scorpions, and over all the power of the enemy; and nothing will hurt you. Nevertheless, do not rejoice at this, that the spirits submit to you, but rejoice that your names are written in heaven"* (Lk 10:17–20).

Point 1. Jesus affirms his disciple's joy; people are now free. He will affirm you.

Point 2. The FSE helps to discern the spirits and deepen intimacy with God.

9. *At that same hour Jesus rejoiced in the Holy Spirit and said, "I thank you, Father, Lord of heaven and earth, because you have hidden these things from the wise and the intelligent and have revealed them to infants; yes, Father, for such was your gracious will"* (Lk 10:21–23).

Point 1. Jesus rejoices with the Spirit and his Father for what is revealed to you.

Point 2. The FSE reveals the true feelings and desires of the Trinity.

10. *Jesus said to his disciples privately, "Blessed are the eyes that see what you see! For I tell you that many prophets and kings desired to see what you see, but did not see it, and to hear what you hear, but did not hear it"* (Lk 10:24).

Point 1. Jesus blesses his disciples' eyes, whispers their gifts. So too with you.

Point 2. The FSE opens eyes and hearts to see and hear God in all things.

The Sending Blessing

Bless my feet, Lord,
as I go out to give the First Spiritual Exercises.
Bless my mind with the confidence to explain it.
Bless my mouth for each exercise I give.
Free me from any anxieties.

Bless my ears to be a good Spiritual Conversation Guide.
Bless my lips to converse with humility.
Bless my heart to discern your movements.
Free me from selfishness.

Bless my eyes to see you at work in my receiver.
Bless my soul with loving reverence for her or him.
Bless my body to feel the rhythms of this retreat.
Free me from distractions.

Bless my hands to be empty of baggage.
Bless my nose to find the holy desires.
Bless my tongue to accept my receiver's hospitality.
Free me from attachments.

Bless my whole self, to be a giver of your peace.
You have freed me for love; now send me.

PART ONE
A Friend of God

THE STORY OF THE FIRST
SPIRITUAL EXERCISES

This is a story you need to know, for you are a part of it. It all began in 1521, at Loyola, a fortified tower in the Basque country. Ignatius read and daydreamed during months of recuperation from a near fatal war wound. It becomes a time of conversion; he desired to give everything away, go to Jerusalem as a penitent pilgrim, and imitate the great saints of the desert. At this time, he wondered at the spirits moving in him, and gave himself over to spiritual conversations with his family.

The next year he set off to the Black Madonna in the mountains of Montserrat where he spent all night in prayer and conversation with her, offering his sword like a knight to become her knight of God. The monks gave him a small book of exercises to help prepare for his confession.

He walked down to Manresa, where he experienced great trials and mystical graces. God taught him about prayer, good and bad spirits, scruples, true desires, creation, and much else. Ignatius wrote his own exercises and discovered that what helps him can help others. He said people "wanted to talk to him, because even though he had no knowledge of spiritual matters, yet in his speech he revealed great fervor and eagerness to go forward in God's service" (*Autobiography* 21). So began the great Ignatian connection between personal relationship, spiritual conversation, and spiritual exercise.

After this, he sailed to Jerusalem but could not stay, so he returned to Barcelona learning Latin for future study. Polanco, an early Jesuit, says that during this time Ignatius did not stop helping many people through his conversations and spiritual exercises.

This continued at Alcalá and Salamanca during his university studies. His conversations attracted the Inquisition, who twice put him in jail, but judged him innocent. He gave exercises from what he now called his little book of Spiritual Exercises, named in this book the FSE, to a noble woman and her daughter, to a baker and his wife, to a hospital orderly, to university professors and students. Young or old, educated or illiterate, poor or rich, Ignatius felt the FSE was for all.

He then started serious studies at the University of Paris. After a year, he also began "to give himself more intensively to spiritual conversations than he normally did, and he gave exercises to three people." At once the three "gave all they had to the poor, even their books" and began begging in the Paris streets (*Autobiography* 77). This caused great commotion at the university and strictures by the authorities. Later a teacher remarked to Ignatius his surprise that no one was causing him trouble anymore. Ignatius answered, "The reason is because I'm not talking to anyone about the things of God. But when the course is over we'll be back to normal!" (*Autobiography* 82).

At this time, Ignatius gave the Spiritual Exercises in a longer form than the FSE, intensively over many months, to his college roommates, Francis Xavier and Pierre Favre. This form of the Exercises, named in this book the Full Spiritual Exercises, had new exercises on decision making, and the life, death, and resurrection of Jesus. Through conversations and regular enjoyable meals, this group of three became a group of seven companions, who all desired to go to Jerusalem and live as actual apostles.

Arriving in Venice, Ignatius "busied himself giving the Exercises and in other spiritual contacts" (*Autobiography* 92). The now nine companions joined him later and while they all waited for a ship, they begged and served in the hospitals. After most were ordained, they went out into the towns, to beg for food, preach on street corners, and engage in spiritual conversations.

When their Jerusalem plans were ended by war, they returned to Rome to offer themselves to the pope. In the end, they became a new religious order, the Society of Jesus. In their Institute, a foundational document for the pope and their new order, they describe their purpose. Not surprisingly, spiritual conversation and giving exercises stand proud in the short list, for these had not only helped so many people but also made them who they were.

Ignatius writes later, "Endeavor to be profitable to individuals by spiritual conversations, by counseling and exhorting to good works, and by conducting spiritual exercises." Again, "The exercises of the first week can be made available to large numbers; and some examinations of conscience and methods of prayer can also be given far more widely, for anyone who has good will seems to be capable of these exercises" (*Constitutions* 84, 649).

In 1548, the pope approved the Spiritual Exercises, and they are printed. In this book were complete instructions and material for giving the Spiritual Exercises in its two full forms, thirty days enclosed from normal life, and thirty weeks in daily life. The book also included instructions for the FSE, given for four weeks in daily life. So there is one book, but three forms of giving the Exercises, which use all or part of the exercises within. Ignatius also includes ways to apply the exercises to different people, their desires, and life situations.

Both the Full and the First Spiritual Exercises were then taken out into Europe and the New World, the FSE being given to greater and greater numbers of people. The early Jesuits record this: Nadal says how different parts of the Exercises helped different people with different needs. Polanco insists the Exercises were intended for every class of society, and in fact had helped every class, in ways that preaching, exhortation, and fear of damnation did not.

Ignatius wrote that the FSE can be extended to large numbers of persons, including women and married ladies. Domenech gave the FSE to orphan boys in Messina. Broet often gave them to young women in Bologna and Landini gave them to priests and young women.[1] Favre saw the FSE ripple through Palma and out into the countryside. As lay and church people received them, they then enthusiastically gave them to others, and these receivers in turn gave them to more others.

One pastoral strategy in a new city seems to have been to give the FSE, then form a lay sodality or confraternity, whose rule of life was a way to live out the exact exercises they had learned and the graces that had been given in the FSE. These sodalities, involving huge numbers, spread like wild fire, and today, 450 years later, they continue as the worldwide Christian Life Community.

The preached Spiritual Exercises, annual retreats for religious, exercises and catechesis, renewal programs, detailed retreat books applying the Exercises to new groups, directories for eight-day versions, drama, music, street processions, art and architecture, devotional books, local language translations, engraved gospel contemplations, visual exercise handouts, the illustrated Exercises and bestselling spirituality books all grew naturally from the seedbed of the Spiritual Exercises. Many of these were locked into the life of Jesuit institutions and missions, which protected the form of the Exercises. Others were creative forms that have flourished and passed, rightly as times, needs, and the world changes.

In the last fifty years, the Spiritual Exercises has seen a new growth of individual spiritual direction in the Full Spiritual Exercises, lay people receiving and giving them, and new forms of street, youth, and guided retreats in daily life. Now the FSE, applied today in full exercise and retreat form, is gathering momentum. In fact, you are a part of it. This is happening now.

Jesuit Congregations, formal international meetings to keep the direction and ministries of the Jesuit order responsive to the greatest needs worldwide, met in 1890 and 1920, and vigorously supported, to the "greatest extent possible," giving the FSE especially to men, ecclesiastics, the workers, and the poor. So too, they encouraged forming sodalities for students, young people, workers, and the poor. Both works, likely in turn, were to "imbue an interior spirit of the Christian life, strengthen in solid virtue, train in love and the works of mercy, and inflame with zeal for souls."[2]

Today the Spiritual Exercises are promoted as a source of similar inspiration, so that "our deep love of God and our passion for his world should set us on fire, a fire that starts other fires."[3] The FSE needs you to take it to wider groups of people again, to new places, to train new givers and recover the great good they can do. In short, use the FSE to light a fire that starts other fires.

In the new millennium, the First Spiritual Exercises is defined again here, to help you describe it to those interested in becoming your receiver of it, and to help you to apply it to her or him in the giving of it.

The Forms of the Exercises

An Ignatian "spiritual exercise" is a five-part structured prayer with a particular aim to bring one into relationship with God. The "Spiritual Exercises" is a set of spiritual exercises, structured in a four-week retreat, with a particular dynamic written by St. Ignatius and developed by his experience, the experience of the first givers, and the experience of those who received it. They are a single, progressive, and powerful experience of grace, built around prayer and spiritual conversation or direction.

The Spiritual Exercises take two forms, the "First" Spiritual Exercises and the "Full" Spiritual Exercises. As noted already, the Full Spiritual Exercises are given for thirty days in seclusion or thirty weeks in daily life. The First Spiritual Exercises are given for four weeks in daily life. The

First Spiritual Exercises, formally called the 18th Annotation Exercises, are "first" in four ways:

1. First in the spiritual journey. They are the first spiritual exercises learnt by the pilgrim Ignatius seeking God's will. They are the first spiritual exercises he gave to others. They are the first exercises you might give to a searcher today.

2. First in content. They contain many "first" exercises: the first principle and foundation, first Christian prayers, first virtues, first morning thoughts, first creation, first sin, first methods of prayer, first fruits of the Spirit, first rules of discernment, etc.

3. First in the dynamic of the Exercises. One of the First Spiritual Exercises retreats includes all of the First Week of the Full Spiritual Exercises. These and other first exercises must be made first before all the rest.

4. First in use. It is the first form of the Spiritual Exercises ever given. It can be given immediately to everyone. It is a complete form of the Spiritual Exercises in its own right. In Ignatian spirituality, it is the best place to begin.

The FSE offers a choice of four retreats to meet different desires. Applying the Exercises to needs and situations today, each retreat guides a person or group through four weeks of prayer in daily life, Monday to Thursday, and includes a Sunday Eucharist and exercise. Fourteen methods of prayer are taught, usually three new methods each retreat. Four Examen prayers, the mini-discernment of spirits, spiritual conversation and a Program for Life are also received.

While these elements are common, the purpose, content, and dynamic of each retreat is different.

Inner Peace in Divine Love. This retreat expands the spiritual exercise called the Contemplation to Attain Divine Love (*Spiritual Exercises* 230–37). In content, it explores a lover's relationship, where each desires to give and receive from the other. It begins with the receiver's experience of love and moves into the gifts of God's love.

Inner Peace in Darkness and Light. This retreat is for those living in some form of darkness, a serious disorder in life, suffering, sinfulness, chronic illness, or lack of freedom. In content, it begins with love, covers the first week of the Full Spiritual Exercises on mercy, gives parallel exercises for

healing, and ends with the freedom exercise known as the Foundation
(*Spiritual Exercises* 23, 45–90).

Inner Peace in Friendship with Jesus. This retreat deepens a friendship
with Jesus. While it is not from Ignatius, a modern reading of the FSE
includes this retreat.

Inner Peace in Service of God. This retreat begins with profoundly beautiful ways of praying using breath and body. Then it considers service,
through the Beatitudes, new commandments, virtues, senses, gifts of the
Spirit, and works of mercy. It uses the three methods of prayer at the end
of the Exercises (*Spiritual Exercises* 238–60).

The FSE story continues today with you and your receiver. It all begins
with receiving and giving, as written in the Letter of 1 Peter:

> Like good stewards of the manifold grace of God, serve one another
> with whatever gift each of you has received. Whoever speaks must do
> so as one speaking the very words of God; whoever serves must do so
> with the strength that God supplies, so that God may be glorified in all
> things through Jesus Christ. (1 Pt 4:10–11)

MOVING WITH INNER PEACE

The purpose of the FSE is to give your receiver deep inner peace. Ignatius says the FSE is for those who desire "a certain level of peace of soul" (*Spiritual Exercises* 18). Elsewhere, Ignatius explains spiritual consolation as "every increase of hope, faith and charity, to all interior happiness which calls and attracts to heavenly things and to the salvation of one's soul, leaving the soul quiet and at peace in her Creator and Lord" (*Spiritual Exercises* 316).

There is a clear connection of a "certain peace of soul" with the consolation "that leaves the soul quiet and at peace in her Creator." So the peace received through the FSE is actually a gift of spiritual consolation, which is a constellation of graces, or a ground of being—no small thing.

In writing about the spirits, Ignatius reveals the many faces of inner peace. It is described as light, peace, tranquility, and quiet. It encompasses a strong, calm self-confidence filled with hope, faith, and love. It is active, uplifting, and zealous for the good (*Spiritual Exercises* 317, 333).

After receiving the FSE, your receiver continues to discern the way forward, following the good spirit and receiving the gifts of consolation and peace. This is what is meant by "moving with inner peace": your receiver walks in spiritual consolation. No matter the ups and downs of life, she or he remains quietly open to the action of God.

For Ignatius, a life of deep sacred peace calls one into love. "The Peace of our Lord is something interior, and it brings with it all the other gifts and graces necessary for salvation and eternal life. This peace makes us love our neighbor for the love of our Creator and Lord" (Letter 1:162).[4]

Love, in turn, leads to the connection between peace and compassion. "For the mountains may depart and the hills be removed, but my steadfast love shall not depart from you, and my covenant of peace shall not be removed, says the Lord, who has compassion on you" (Is 54:10). When Jesus responds with compassion, he is "moved" to give inner peace as a second gift.

Thus he heals the woman with the chronic hemorrhage, saying, "Daughter, your faith has made you well; go in peace, and be healed of your disease" (Mk 5:34). He forgives the woman who was a sinner, saying, "Your faith has saved you; go in peace" (Lk 7:50). And in the presence of fear, when the disciples felt their boat was sinking, he says to the wind and sea, "Peace, Be still!" (Mk 4:39).

This double gift of Jesus is built into the FSE. Six gifts are sought in four retreats. With each grace given, your receiver begins to move with inner peace:

1. The first gift is unconditional love.

   Peace moves in profound gratitude.

2. The second gift is forgiveness.

   Peace moves in pure wonder.

3. The third gift is healing.

   Peace moves in divine intimacy.

4. The fourth gift is freedom.

   Peace moves in deep reverence.

5. The fifth gift is friendship with Jesus.

   Peace moves in quiet joy.

6. The sixth gift is service.

   Peace moves in great energy.

On maintaining peace, Ignatius, in a letter to St. Francis Borgia, writes:

> I would deem it preferable to convert half your time (from inner exercises) into study, to administration of your estates and spiritual conversations, always taking care to maintain your soul in peace, quiet, and readiness for whenever Our Lord might wish to work in it. (Letter 466)

SENT WITH THE FIRST
SPIRITUAL EXERCISES

The ministry of the FSE is like a hand with its five fingers. At the end of a retreat, invite your receiver to help others through the first three parts of the ministry listed below. She or he, through the graces and skills already received, could begin these immediately. The remaining two are beautiful ways for your receiver to continue the divine relationships enjoyed in the FSE, and enrich all his or her other relationships to great effect. So, at the end of giving an FSE retreat, you are like Jesus, inviting and sending your receiver out to make a difference. The handful of FSE ministries are:

1. to give the FSE to large numbers of people,

2. to have a Program for Life,

3. to converse spiritually,

4. to go forward peacefully, and

5. to live in friendship with the Lord.

To give the FSE to large numbers of people: This is the thumb, the universal sign of agreement and go-ahead. The FSE was created to reach large numbers of people. With no special requirements, the FSE can be given widely. Anyone who has prayed one of the exercises and received the graces of that exercise, can teach it to another. Some more, with training, may become givers of FSE retreats.

To have a Program for Life: This is the index finger, the searching and identifying finger. The Program for Life identifies ways to keep graces alive, balance life commitments, and choose personal acts to help others.

To converse spiritually: The is the middle finger. Conversations take place in the middle of everything else. Spiritual conversations give new life. People yearn for deeper, reverential conversations. The world, too, and Christian communities, desperately need the collective wisdom of the Christian group and its Spirit, in order to find new and better ways forward.

To go forward peacefully: This is the ring finger, sign of love and fidelity to the Spirit, and the Spirit's commitment to help your receiver to move "in courage and strength, consolations, inspirations and quiet, making things easy and removing all obstacles" (*Spiritual Exercises* 315). It is a way of life.

To live in friendship with the Lord: This is the little finger, a sign of a friendship that includes even the smallest things. Jesus called his disciples friends because they knew everything he had to reveal. The FSE allows Jesus to share everything he knows again, so your receiver may be his friend and live a loving, fruitful life:

> "I have called you friends, because I have made known to you every-thing that I have heard from my Father. You did not choose me but I chose you. And I appointed you to go and bear fruit, fruit that will last, so that the Father will give you whatever you ask him in my name." (Jn 15:15–16)

DEVELOPING A SUPPORT NETWORK

Here, and following, are five guides to support you in giving the FSE. They also set sensible boundaries and list situations where the appropriate response to help your receiver is to help them find a priest or Christian minister, spiritual director or counselor. With good preparation, such people can both form both a good support network and be a safety net for you. The fifth guide is a code of ethics for the Givers, Mentors, Instructors and Trainers of the FSE.

The FSE has a "Rule of Two" and this will be your first powerful, practical, and spiritual support. It takes this rule from the actions and advice of both Jesus and Ignatius. Jesus sent his disciples out in pairs. Ignatius writes, "It would be wise when possible not to send one person by himself, but instead at least two persons, so that they might be of greater aid to one another in spiritual and bodily matters, and also, by dividing up among themselves the labors in the service of their neighbor, be of more benefit to those to whom they are sent" (*Constitutions* 624). He adds the values of matching complementary talents, balancing characters, and sending the more experienced with the less. So having a companion in training, a partner in giving an FSE retreat, and a mentor to begin with will give you support and enhance the quality of both your understanding and your giving of an FSE retreat.

In practice, the FSE will nearly always be given in partnership with a local Christian community or interest group. A normal part of planning, preparing, giving, and follow up will be negotiation, sharing, and co-work with that local community's leaders, ministers, structures, and ways of proceeding.

So the FSE is consciously seeded in the lives, ministries, and communal groups of the local community. It always aims to serve. It is not about setting up a new group in opposition or in competition of scare resources in a local church or community. So the approach and explanation of the

FSE to local leaders is crucially important to receive the support needed to give the FSE.

Mentor, Retreat Team, FSE Community

While the FSE may be profitably given one to one, the normal way will be by a group of Givers. If you are giving the FSE to just one other person, or giving it for the first time, a Mentor is highly recommended. A Mentor is a Giver of the FSE who is greatly experienced and well trained to mentor you.

If you belong to a group of Givers of the FSE and are giving a retreat to a large group, or number of small groups, your natural support and help will be the group of fellow Givers. If you are working with such a group, you will find great support and encouragement in working with the local leaders and resource people to ground the FSE in that community. There is wider support to be found in regional groups of those working with the FSE and in the international community of the FSE, which will be developed online.

When to seek help:

In the preparation, giving and review of the FSE retreat. Help should be sought as needed for guidance, support, information, a receiver in need, and a group of concern.

Where to get help:

1. FSE partner

2. FSE mentor

3. FSE retreat team

4. FSE online community

What does an FSE retreat team do?

An FSE retreat team is that group of trained people who are planning, advertising, coordinating, giving, and following up the FSE with a community or individuals.

Things to remember:
Seek a mentor through your FSE training course. If one is unavailable, ask a good friend for regular conversations at preset times over the four weeks. These conversations should be on your experience as giver, not the confidential experience of your receiver.

What do I need to do to have a good support network?
Before you give the FSE in a particular area, a part of your training, preparation, and support network will be to have a mentor if you are a beginner, and a partner or team to help give the FSE. The FSE website may also help, or pre-arranged support via Skype, phone, or e-mail. Do this before you give the FSE in a particular area.

Priests and Ministers

You will need to liaise with your local churches and their priests, ministers, or pastoral associates as a matter of courtesy and for support, especially with the FSE exercises that include the sacraments and the Sunday Eucharist.

Furthermore, many local churches have spirituality ministries, prayer groups, men's groups, women's groups, service groups, and pastoral associates who would be happy to work with you.

When to seek help:

Before you begin the FSE, you need to be able to direct your receiver to a local parish or congregation and inform him or her about the availability of the Eucharist and the Sacraments of Reconciliation and Anointing of the Sick. There you will also find useful resources for the Program for Life exercise. Priests, ministers and pastoral associates are trained and called to help people in the areas of pastoral care and adult faith formation and all the pastoral issues these contexts involve. Refer your receiver to them for urgent pastoral needs during the FSE. Adult faith formation and general needs should only be explored after the retreat.

Where to get help:

1. Local priests and ministers

2. Local pastoral associates

3. Diocesan or regional pastoral coordinators

4. Lay Christian communities and initiatives

What does a priest or minister do?

Priests and ministers are ordained by their church to provide spiritual, sacramental, communal, and pastoral care to their people. Pastoral associates assist or specialize in one of these areas. Both will be well experienced with helping people at the important times of their lives whether they be births, marriage, family celebrations, family crises, or deaths.

Things to remember:
The local church is the Body of Christ. The people and ministers serve to build and nurture this community. Christian communal identity is something your receiver may only slowly appreciate. Indeed, your receiver might be called to create new forms of Christian community.

What do I need to do to receive support from the local Christian community?
Before you give the FSE in a particular area make up a list of local churches of all denominations and their priests and ministers, pastoral associates, spirituality groups, lay Christian initiatives, and web resources.

Spiritual Directors

Spiritual direction may be seen as rest stops in the journey of life, places where one can receive reverence, attentive listening, spiritual guidance, and professional support.

When to seek help:

The inner journey of your receiver changes as her or his relationship with God grows. Ignatius notes that times of great confusion, obstacles, strong feelings pulling in many directions, darkness, or simply being stuck may be best discerned with the help of a spiritual director.

The same is true when your receiver has powerful moments of divine intimacy, mysterious prayer experiences, vocational calls to serve particular people, or an important life decision to make. The spiritual director offers clear spiritual direction, encouragement, and the best of Christian wisdom.

Where to get help:

1. Retreat or spirituality centers, such as through the Society of Jesus (Jesuits) or another religious community in your area.

2. Trained lay spiritual directors through local spirituality centers, the Internet, Spiritual Directors International, or another professional association of spiritual directors.

3. Spiritual guides in local churches of all denominations or other Christian communities.

What does a spiritual director do?

Spiritual direction is a one-to-one relationship where, in regular meetings, the director listens to the prayer experience of the directee. Both seek to understand how God is working in the life and prayer of the directee. The director gives prayer guides and practical helps. Spiritual directors may also be called spiritual companions or guides. Only choose those with professional training.

Things to remember:
A spiritual director is trained to look at movements of the Spirit in prayer and daily life. An Ignatian spiritual director is also trained to see movements of spiritual consolation and desolation. Both can offer your receiver practical guidelines for life directions and important decisions.

What do I need to do to be ready to help my receiver find a spiritual director?
Before you give the FSE make up a list of local spiritual directors, spirituality centers, web contacts, etc.

Counselors

All the spiritual exercises in the FSE draw on a receiver's life experience, which includes their memories and feelings with those experiences. The exercises also encourage receivers to honestly come to the God who loves them just as they are and to express their deepest desires. Sometimes these desires and feelings have been buried under considerable suffering. This means exercises can uncover experiences and memories that are hard to deal with alone. Here a counselor can be of great help.

As a giver of the FSE and Spiritual Conversation Guide you may notice when a receiver is in difficulty, but you are not a counselor. Rather, as you might with a family member or friend, you can gently ask them if they need help at this time and guide them to where they can get that help.

When to suggest your receiver seek help:
Among the issues that may require a professional counselor are abuse (physical or emotional), anger management, anxiety disorders, depression, grief, life crisis, trauma, and violence.

Where to get help:
1. Your receiver's local doctor

2. Local community health center

3. Lifeline or similar crisis help lines

4. Christian family and social-service organizations

5. Diocesan and regional mental-health and counseling

6. Christian counseling associations

7. Government mental-health services and foundations

8. National registers of psychotherapists and counselors

What does a counselor do?

"A counselor is a trained professional who can help you work out your personal problems. The counselor helps you to resolve your problems in a positive way by helping you to clarify the issues, explore options, develop strategies and increase self-awareness. Counseling is usually a short-term treatment for a specific problem."[5]

Things to remember:

The above organizations, groups, and services all have websites.

What do I need to do to be ready to help my receiver find a counselor?

Before you give the FSE make up a list of local doctors, counselors, therapists, Christian social services, local health services, and web resources.

Code of Ethics

This code of ethics for givers of the First Spiritual Exercises is based on the code of ethics of The Companions in the Ministry of the Ignatian Spiritual Exercises in Australia.

Why do givers of the First Spiritual Exercises need a Code of Ethics?

Norms for ethical conduct in the ministry of the First Spiritual Exercises are essential today because of the requirement of public accountability. This code provides behavioral standards for the giver of the FSE. This code of ethics is also for Trainers, Instructors and Mentors of the FSE.

Terms used:

The description "First Spiritual Exercises" is abbreviated FSE.

The one giving the FSE to another is called the *giver*. The one making an FSE retreat is called the *receiver*.

The form of guided reflection after prayer in the FSE is called *spiritual conversation*. It requires training.

The one guiding the giver of the FSE during his or her initial retreats is called the *Mentor*.

The one teaching single spiritual exercises is called an *instructor*.

The one who trains a giver of the FSE is called a *trainer*.

The above terms are made in distinction from the terms used for the Full Spiritual Exercises. There, the one giving the Full Spiritual Exercises is called the *spiritual director*. The one making the Full Exercises is called the *exercitant* or *retreatant*. The form of guided reflection after prayer in the Full Exercises is called *spiritual direction*. It requires professional training.

1. How do givers of the FSE act responsibly toward themselves?

   (a) They consider or maintain responsible association with their own faith community.

   (b) They maintain their own life of faith and prayer with ongoing spiritual conversation.

   (c) They receive appropriate mentoring.

   (d) They consult other appropriately qualified persons when necessary.

2. How do givers of the FSE act responsibly toward receivers?

   (a) Givers of the FSE discuss with prospective receivers:

      (i) The nature of the FSE;

      (ii) The respective roles of the giver and the receiver;

      (iii) The length and frequency of spiritual conversation sessions;

      (iv) Confidentiality and its limitations;

      (v) Freedom of both parties to terminate the relationship.

   (b) Givers of the FSE will work under a mentor in giving the FSE retreats for the first time.

   (c) Givers of the FSE do not give the FSE for cost or financial gain. What was freely received by givers (the FSE) is freely given to others.

   (d) Givers of the FSE limit the number of receivers they accept to that which is reasonably possible, either individually or in a group.

   (e) Givers of the FSE will help receivers to seek a qualified priest or minister, pastoral associate, spiritual director, or counselor when asked for or needed.

   (f) Givers of the FSE who have other professional qualifications and clients (such as counselors) ensure that they clarify with the receiver the nature of their relationship as a giver of the FSE.

   (g) A giver of the FSE respects the dignity of the receiver by:

(i) respecting the receiver's life story, values, conscience, spirituality, and theology;

(ii) limiting inquiry into the personal life of the receiver to those matters directly relevant to the making of the FSE;

(iii) recognizing the unequal power relationship between a giver of the FSE and the receiver and acting to avoid exploitation;

(iv) refraining from behavior that is sexualized, manipulative, abusive, or coercive; and

(v) maintaining appropriate physical and psychological boundaries.

(h) A giver of the FSE respects the privacy of the receiver by:

(i) protecting the identity of the receiver, and the fact that he or she is receiving the FSE;

(ii) keeping confidential all personal communications and making no written notes; keeping confidential information from spiritual conversation groups that reveal the identy of the person;

(iii) not giving or receiving from givers, mentors, spiritual directors, professionals, or ministers information about their receiver without her or his written permission;

(iv) conducting spiritual-conversation meetings in an appropriate location;

(v) ensuring that both the giver and the receiver of the FSE are aware of any legal requirements that may override confidentiality, including, but not limited to, provisions about child abuse, sexual assault of children or adults, elder abuse and physical harm to self and others, and other criminal behaviors.

3. How do givers of the FSE act responsibly toward faith communities?

(a) Givers of the FSE are sensitive to the faith traditions to which their receivers belong.

(b) Givers of the FSE do not engage in any proselytizing that is directed toward changing the commitment of a receiver to the giver's faith community.

(c) Givers of the FSE respect the processes of decision making, accountability, and support offered by faith communities.

4. How do givers of the FSE act responsibly toward society?

(a) Givers of the FSE represent their qualifications accurately in any public communication.

(b) Givers of the FSE do not make statements that contain any of the following:

> (i) a false, fraudulent, misleading, deceptive, or unfair statement;

> (ii) a misrepresentation of fact or a statement likely to mislead or deceive because in context it makes only a partial disclosure of relevant facts;

> (iii) a testimonial from a receiver, without permission of that receiver, regarding the quality of spiritual conversation received from the giver of the FSE;

> (iv) a statement intended to or likely to create false or unjustified expectations of favorable results of making the FSE;

> (v) a statement implying unusual, unique, or one-of-a-kind abilities, including misrepresentation through sensationalism, exaggeration, or superficiality;

> (vi) a statement intended to or likely to exploit a receiver's fears, anxieties, or emotions;

> (vii) a statement about the comparative desirability of the spiritual conversation offered; or

> (viii) a statement of direct solicitation of individual receivers.

(c) Givers of the FSE conform to legislation requiring the disclosure of information to public authorities in cases of abuse, danger, or crime.

PART TWO

A Spiritual CONVERSATION Guide

SPEAKING ABOUT THE THINGS
OF GOD

Spiritual conversation is less about the content of a conversation than it is about the relationship between the two people speaking and listening. While spiritual things make for spiritual conversations, what really makes a conversation "spiritual" is the way each person holds the other in loving reverence as they converse. Each gives the other person deep respect, each remains humble before the other, and each is open to being moved by the other.

So when Ignatius instructs his men on how to converse, he begins with the humble awareness of the other, including the awareness that Jesus gave his life for the person conversing with them.

This is why he focuses on aims, means, and relationships in conversation. Little is said of particular content. This is left to preaching, teaching catechism and sacred lectures. As a Spiritual Conversation Guide you need to understand that spiritual conversation is none of these.

Rather, Ignatius would encourage *acatamiento*, awe and reverence of the other. This is a way pointed out to him by God, one he wished to take forever. You can see this in these excerpts from his spiritual diary:

> I had a steady thought which penetrated the depth of my soul; How great is the reverence and affectionate awe with which I ought pronounce the name of God our Lord, and so on; and further, that I ought to seek, not tears, but this affectionate awe and reverence. (*Spiritual Diary* 156)

> I became convinced of this, I ought to attach a greater value to this grace and knowledge than to all other past graces. . . . I had found the way which was being pointed out to me. It seemed to be the best of all and the one I ought follow always. (*Spiritual Diary* 157, 162)

> I kept on thinking that humility, reverence, and affectionate awe ought to be not fearful but loving. This took root in my mind so deeply that I begged over and over again: "Give me loving humility, and with it

35

reverence and affectionate awe." (*Spiritual Diary* 178–79)

It seemed to me that I ought not stop there, but that the same would apply in relation to creatures: that is to say, loving humility and all it brings would so apply. . . . During these periods of time, on several occasions I had a vision of the divine being in circular shape. (*Spiritual Diary* 180)

As a giver of the FSE and Spiritual Conversation Guide, your primary stance before your receiver may best be described as loving reverence, awe, and humility. This is also the stance you ask of each receiver toward the other receivers, where all converse in the circle of God.

Indeed, Ignatius would have you and your receiver converse like Jesus:

Let no one seek to be considered a clever talker, or pride himself on being polished, witty and well spoken; he should look at Christ, who despised all this and chose for our sakes to be humiliated and looked down on by people rather than honored and esteemed. (Letter 11)[6]

Over time a connection grows for Ignatius between speaking about the things of God and giving exercises. What he receives, he shares with others. You will see this by reading these selections from his *Autobiography*. They show his early ministry of spiritual conversation and exercises. (The places where Ignatius was at the time are in italic type.)

Loyola. With no worry at all, I persevered in my reading and my good resolutions; and all my time of conversation with members of the household I spent on the things of God; thus I benefited their souls. As I very much liked those books, the idea came to me to note down briefly some of the more essential things from the life of Christ and the saints, so I set myself very diligently to write a book. . . . Part of the time I spent in writing and part in prayer. (*Autobiography* 11)

Manresa. After I began to be consoled by God, and saw the fruit which I bore in dealing with souls, I gave up those extremes I had formerly practiced, and I now cut my nails and my hair. At this time there was a long period during which I was eager to converse on spiritual matters and to find persons who could deal with them. (*Autobiography* 29)

Venice. A rich Spaniard took me home to dinner, and kept me for a few days. Ever since Manresa I had the habit when I ate with anyone, never to speak at table except to answer briefly; but I listened to what was said and noted some things which I took as the occasion to speak about God, and when the meal was finished, I did so. This was the reason why the worthy gentleman and all his household were so attached to me and wanted me to stay. (*Autobiography* 42–43)

Alcalá. While at Alcalá, I was engaged in giving spiritual exercises and teaching Christian doctrine, and this bore fruit for the glory of God. There were many persons who came to a deep understanding and relish of spiritual things. . . . A policeman put me in jail (on the orders of the inquisitors). This was in summertime, and as I was not confined, many people came to visit me. I did the same things as when I was free, teaching and giving exercises. (*Autobiography* 57, 60)

Salamanca. "Well, then, what do you preach?" "We do not preach," I said, "but we do speak familiarly with some people about the things of God; for example, after dinner with some people who invite us." "But" said the friar, "what things of God do you speak about? That is just what we would like to know." "We speak," I said, "sometimes of one virtue, sometimes of another, and do so, praising it; sometimes of one vice, sometimes of another, condemning it." (*Autobiography* 65)

Salamanca. When our imprisonment (myself and Calisto) was known in the city, people sent to the jail something on which we could sleep and all that was needed, in abundance. And always there was a crowd to visit us, and I kept up this practice of speaking about God, etc. (*Autobiography* 67)

Azpetia. In this hospice (near my home) I began to speak with many who came to visit me, of the things of God, by whose grace much fruit was derived. (*Autobiography* 88)

A conversing relationship is fundamental to prayer, uncovering desires, personal change, decision making, community renewal, deepening relationships and the quality of service. So spiritual conversations with your receiver are important, not only about prayer, but also in themselves, since they are inherently necessary for friendship with God and the good of your receiver's neighbor.

One of the first companions of Ignatius, Simon Rodriguez, wrote of him in Paris, "Ignatius understood the art of dealing with persons and of binding them to himself through charming, winning behavior, to a degree which, to be honest, I have never found with anyone else. . . . He could gradually affect their hearts in such a way that, through his behavior, and through his pleasant, gentle speech, he carried all mightily away to the love of God."[7]

The best way to train your receiver in spiritual conversation is for him or her to practice it often. This can be with you, at home, and in daily relationships. If you wish to enrich that training in addition to the retreat exercises, you could give him or her one of the following single exercises. In Inner Peace in Service of God, the exercises on the virtues, fruits of the Spirit, and spiritual works of mercy. In Inner Peace in Friendship with Jesus, the exercises on listening, receiving, and accepting. In Inner Peace in Darkness and Light, the exercises on praise, reverence and service.

There are two additional Ignatian resources on spiritual conversation: "Advanced Guidelines for the Practice of Discernment of Spirits" (pp. 64–67) and "Seven Approaches to Spiritual Conversation" (pp. 68–69).

HOW TO USE THE
LISTENING BOOK

Ignatius describes above how he used his spiritual journal at Loyola and throughout his life. He really listened to what it had to teach him. This regular reflection, and search for patterns of grace, is so Ignatian that a tighter focus and process has been given to the spiritual journal in the FSE, in the creation of the Listening Book.

The Listening Book is a book your receiver listens to after writing his or her reflections in it. Following a spiritual exercise, he or she considers the questions listed below in the first use of the Listening Book. After noting responses in the Listening Book, your receiver then closes it.

After some time, an hour, day or week, your receiver opens it and carefully reads what was written. She or he "listens" to the Listening Book as it reveals new meanings, insights, and feelings. The original prayer experience always has more grace in it than a receiver might realize at first.

Using the Listening Book also gives the inner self and the unconscious self of your receiver time to absorb the prayer experience. It gives the receiver, as well, a way to tell what he or she has discovered. Of course, the Holy Spirit also speaks through a Listening Book.

In the FSE, the Listening Book of your receiver will become the voice of a friend as he or she moves through the full dynamic of the retreat. Practically, ask your receiver to buy a book to have as a Listening Book. Then she or he can title it beautifully and bless it before use.

Ignatius says, "Every day I used to write down what passed through my soul, and so could now find these things in writing" (*Autobiography* 99). The Listening Book will help your receiver to catch and chart what passes through his or her soul.

Apart from use after a spiritual exercise or other prayer, the Listening Book has three other direct uses. The second use is after a spiritual conversation, the third is after praying the Awareness Examen and the fourth is during an important life event. Three of the four uses are outlined in what follows with their own reflection questions. The fourth can take the same reflection questions as the third.

Luis Gonçalves de Câmara writes of Ignatius, "He said to me that as for the Exercises he had not produced them all at one time, rather that some things which he used to observe in his soul and find useful for himself it seemed to him could also be useful for others, and so he used to put them in writing" (*Autobiography* 99). Your receiver's Listening Book will also help her or him to help others. It will contain favorite exercises, graces of understanding, and clues of what the Spirit wishes your receiver to share with others.

1. After a Spiritual Exercise

Preparation	After my spiritual exercise I will reflect on how things have gone in my prayer:
Reflection	What were the more important things in my prayer?
	What were my stronger feelings? What detail gave rise to them?
	Has my relationship with the Lord grown? How? Why?
	Have I received the grace I asked for? Other insights? Delights?
	Have I felt spiritual consolation or desolation since my prayer time?
	Is there action I wish to take?
Listening Book	I note my responses to the above in my Listening Book.
	I return, when I desire, to listen to new revelations from my prayer.

2. After a Spiritual Conversation

Preparation	After finishing the spiritual conversation I reflect on how it has gone:
Reflection	What were the more important things I heard in the spiritual conversation?
	Where was I most engaged? What did I learn?
	What were my stronger feelings? Insights?
	Did any of my desires sharpen or deepen?

Have I felt consolation or desolation since my conversation?

Is there action I wish to take?

Listening Book   I note my responses to the above in my Listening Book.

I return, when I desire, to hear new wisdom from this conversation.

3. After an Awareness Examen

Preparation   After my Awareness Examen, I note the following:

Reflection   For what did I feel gratitude today?

How did God act in my life today?

What life-giving patterns are revealed in the past week?

In what direction is the good spirit leading me? The bad spirit?

Have I felt consolation or desolation since my examen?

Is there action I wish to take?

Listening Book   I note my responses to the above in my Listening Book.

I return, when I desire, to receive new insights from my examen.

HOW TO GUIDE SPIRITUAL CONVERSATION

Contemplative Silence   Listen to the loving Trinity.

1. Listening   Listen to new things received in prayer.

2. Conversation   Conversation on prayer experiences.

3. Discernment   Listen to mini-discernments of the spirits.

Contemplative Silence   Listen to the active Trinity.

Suggested Time: 60 minutes

Silence: 5 minutes. Listening: 15 minutes. Conversation: 25 minutes. Discernment: 10 minutes. Silence: 5 minutes. Time for phases may be adjusted.

During the FSE, the content of spiritual conversation will be about the spiritual exercise, or set of exercises, recently prayed, or about what was noted in the Listening Book, or even about what was just heard. While this guide suits both one or a group of receivers, it will address a group having a spiritual conversation. People new to sitting in contemplative silence might begin to remain in the presence of the Trinity by just feeling their breath, or listening to external sounds, for the whole time of silence.

Contemplative silence begins the conversation—out of the busy world into the sacred now:

> *I begin with eyes closed, to focus on the feeling of my breath as it passes through my nostrils. I do this for two minutes. . . . Then I imagine the Trinity, sitting in a close circle with me, as four friends do in a conversation. I imagine talk has stopped and they are just loving me unconditionally. . . . I remain in this silent loving presence for three minutes. . . . When distracted, I return to the circle by praying, "Thank you. I accept your love."*

After this silence, there are three phases:

The first phase is sacred listening. Here each shares something of his or her prayer experience, if desired. Everyone listens as detailed in "The Practice of Sacred Listening."

The second phase is spiritual conversation. Here the group converses about the graces experienced in prayer and daily life, in the way Ignatius advises in "The Practice of Spiritual Conversation" (pp. 54–55).

The third phase is discernment of spirits. Here each is each invited to share briefly any mini-discernment as in "The Practice of Discernment of Spirits" (pp. 60–67), Everyone just listens.

Contemplative silence ends the conversation—joining the working Trinity to return to the world:

> *I close my eyes. . . . I imagine the active Trinity sitting in an intimate circle with me . . . I listen to the Father, Jesus and Spirit express their desire to work with and through me. I sit in silence with their invitation. If distracted I return to the circle by praying, "Yes, work through me." I remain here in silent presence for three minutes. . . . Now I listen to the sounds surrounding me . . . near and far, loud and quiet. After two minutes of listening to the active world, I end with opening my eyes and a Sign of the Cross.*

In the discernment of spirits phase, you need to be very clear with your receivers that there is no discussion of another's experience of the spirits. Rather, the group returns to listening, like in the first phase, to appreciate with affectionate awe and reverence how the good spirit works in each.

Finally, this highly structured way of spiritual conversation is just that—a structured, experiential way of learning—an exercise or practice. Spiritual conversations have a free-flowing vitality and weave of feelings, mystery and story. The structure of the spiritual exercise here simply gives such life a chance to sprout and develop roots.

Phase One: Sacred Listening

Silence creates the space for listening. Silence also allows one to simply be, simply be in the now, simply be in the presence of the other. Contemplative silence is simply being in the presence of God. Similarly, contemplative silence can be found in the presence of a person or a group of people. Good spiritual conversation starts with silence and then moves to listening in silence.

God tries to tell this to Job, "Pay heed, Job, listen to me; be silent, and I will speak. If you have anything to say, answer me; speak, for I desire to justify you. If not, listen to me; be silent, and I will teach you wisdom" (Jb 33:31–33).

And God explains to Isaiah that to listen is to receive life, that listening is like eating, "Listen carefully to me, and eat what is good, and delight yourselves in rich food. Incline your ear, and come to me; listen, so that you may live" (Is 55:2–3).

There are three Bible stories that break open sacred listening. They each tell different truths. Three points follow each story for you and your receiver to ponder.

Speak Lord; Your Servant Is Listening

At that time Eli, whose eyesight had begun to grow dim so that he could not see, was lying down in his room; the lamp of God had not yet gone out, and Samuel was lying down in the temple of the Lord, where the ark of God was. Then the Lord called, "Samuel! Samuel!" and he said, "Here I am!" and ran to Eli, and said, "Here I am, for you called me." But he said, "I did not call; lie down again." So he went and lay down. The Lord called again, "Samuel!" Samuel got up and went to Eli, and said, "Here I am, for you called me." But he said, "I did not call, my son; lie down again." Now Samuel did not yet know the Lord, and the word of the Lord had not yet been revealed to him. The Lord called Samuel again, a third time. And he got up and went to Eli, and said, "Here I am, for you called me." Then Eli perceived that the Lord was calling the boy. Therefore Eli said to Samuel, "Go, lie down; and if he calls you, you shall say, 'speak, Lord, for your servant is listening.'"

So Samuel went and lay down in his place. Now the Lord came and stood there, calling as before, "Samuel! Samuel!" And Samuel said, "Speak, for your servant is listening." Then the Lord said to Samuel,

"See, I am about to do something in Israel that will make both ears of anyone who hears of it tingle." (1 Sm 3:2–11)

Point 1. Samuel sleeps in a sacred place yet knows not the Lord.

Point 2. He is called by name three times, by a voice both mysterious and intimate.

Point 3. He takes a humble position for conversation, a servant listening to his Lord.

The Sound of Sheer Silence

The word of the Lord came to Elijah, "Go out and stand on the mountain before the Lord, for the Lord is about to pass by." Now there was a great wind, so strong that it was splitting mountains and breaking rocks in pieces before the Lord, but the Lord was not in the wind; and after the wind an earthquake, but the Lord was not in the earthquake; and after the earthquake a fire, but the Lord was not in the fire; and after the fire a sound of sheer silence. When Elijah heard it, he wrapped his face in his mantle and went out and stood at the entrance of the cave. Then there came a voice to him that said, "What are you doing here, Elijah?" (1 Kgs 19:9, 11)

Point 1. Elijah assumes that the Lord will come in great displays of might.

Point 2. But the Lord comes in the sound of sheer silence.

Point 3. Now Elijah is really listening. He comes out of his cave. A conversation begins.

Mary Has Chosen the Better Part

Jesus entered a certain village, where a woman named Martha welcomed him into her home. She had a sister named Mary, who sat at the Lord's feet and listened to what he was saying. But Martha was distracted by her many tasks; so she came to him and asked, "Lord, do you not care that my sister has left me to do all the work by myself? Tell her then to help me." The Lord answered her, "Martha, Martha, you are worried and distracted by many things; there is need of only one thing. Mary has chosen the better part, which will not be taken away from her. (Lk 10:38–42)

Point 1. Mary is in a listening relationship with Jesus—quiet, receptive and focused.

Point 2. Martha is in a serving relationship with Jesus—but annoyed, closed and distracted.

Point 3. Jesus affirms that Mary has chosen the better part. The work of listening comes first.

To teach your receiver sacred listening, begin with consideration of the three stories above. Then take your receiver through "The Practice of Sacred Listening," with examples from the experience of reverent listening that you both have. Then it is a matter of practice. Ask your receiver to practice sacred listening at home, at work, with family, friends and strangers, and with you in the retreat.

The Practice of Sacred Listening

Practices 1–9 are from *The Top Ten Powerful Listening Practices* (The Listening Center[8]). Practices 10–12 are from the author.

1. Listen and stop talking.

    One person speaks at a time. One of the most irritating listening habits is that of interrupting.

2. Listen before speaking.

    Allow the person who is speaking time to complete his or her thought, and then wait a few seconds before responding. Or ask, "Is there anything else?" There almost always is.

3. Listen to yourself.

    Be in touch with your inner voice. Ask yourself, "What wants to be said next?"

4. Listen with an open mind.

    Be curious and appreciative of what you are listening to. Listen for new ideas instead of judging and evaluating.

5. Listen for understanding.

    You do not have to agree with what you hear, or even believe it, in order to listen to understand the other person.

6. Listen and ask for clarification.

    If you do not understand what someone is saying, just ask.

7. Listen with empathy and compassion.

    Put your agenda aside. Suspend assumptions. Put yourself in their shoes.

8. Listen with patience and presence.

    Listening well takes time and your full "listening presence."

9. Listen in relationship. Let the speaker know that you have heard them.

    Use your body language: nodding, facial expressions and eye contact.

10. Listen for the Creator reflected in the other.

    Every person is created in the image of God. Reverence the divine in them. Everyone has equal status. Be a servant to the voice you hear. (*Spiritual Exercises* 3, 39, 114, 235)

11. Listen for the Spirit at work in the other.

    Listen for the Spirit who touches the soul of the other "gently, lightly, and sweetly, like a drop of water going into a sponge." (*Spiritual Exercises* 236, 335)

12. Listen for Jesus addressing me through the other.

    The friendship Jesus offers is communal, one vine but many branches. Jesus may speak to you from the graces of another. Listen with just such expectation.

Litany for Listeners

Dearest Lord, here we are, listening as you desire.
Open our ears, our whole being,
that we may become a listening presence to each other,
and enjoy the gift of our spiritual conversation.

Give us the generosity to listen with openness	Listen to us.
the wisdom to understand what is heard	Listen to us.
the strength to be changed by what is shared	Listen to us.
the listening that never judges	Listen to us.
the curiosity of a child	Listen to us.
Increase in us the peace to forgive and be forgiven	Listen to us.
the grace to honor both loss and gift	Listen to us.
the acceptance that allows failure to be shared	Listen to us.
the prudence to know when not to speak	Listen to us.
the surrender that treasures silence after word	Listen to us.
Ground in us the freedom that allows mystery	Listen to us.
the joy to celebrate new things found	Listen to us.
the readiness for laughter when it rises	Listen to us.
the reverence to listen with humble love	Listen to us.
the awe to hear you speaking in us	Listen to us.

Thank you. Amen.

Phase Two: Spiritual Conversation

Sacred listening, reverent conversation and simple discernment of spirits combine to create good spiritual conversations. In all three, speakers and listeners seek to understand how God is at work in their prayer and daily life. This is a very particular focus. It is not about teaching, proselytizing, or counseling. It is about seeking and finding God in all things. For Ignatius, the spirit of such conversation is clear: be slow to speak, listen quietly, treat others as equals, be humble and sincere, speak with kindness and love, be reverent and see the Trinity at work in all.

Spiritual conversation has two places in the FSE. It is used during the retreat to guide your receiver, and it is carried on afterward by your receiver in his or her daily relationships. This means spiritual conversation is more than just a process in a retreat, it is a ministry that is first learned and experienced in the FSE and then practiced after the retreat. Thinking about where good spiritual conversations go adds depth and meaning to spiritual conversations in the FSE.

Although confidentiality is very necessary for spiritual conversation among receivers during the retreat, it is not absolute in the sense that nothing at all will be shared with people outside that group. On the contrary, what your receiver learns, and is energized about, is surely to be shared with as many people as it will help. Indeed, the Spirit will begin with the desires of your receiver, work with them in the prayer exercises, enrich them in the following spiritual conversations—all with the larger intention of helping others through your receiver much later.

Ignatius goes even further. He singles out three kinds of people for the ministry of spiritual conversation: those in greater need, those who are influential, and those who could help others. "They should be the ones from whom the most results can be foreseen, supposing he cannot deal with everybody. Such would be persons in greatest need and those possessing great authority, learning or temporal goods, and others who are suited to be laborers, in general those who, if helped themselves, would most be able to help others, for God's glory" (Letter 24).[9] Your receivers are especially found in the last category. They will better help others.

So the spiritual conversation is as important as the prayer. This is the way graces spread. This is the way receivers experience community at the level of faith, perhaps for the first time. This is the way receivers become multipliers, witnesses, and even instructors of exercises. As Ignatius says,

"Associating and dealing with many people for the salvation and spiritual progress of souls can be very profitable with God's help" (Letter 123).

After being healed, the Geresene demonic, a blind man and others express to Jesus their strong desire to follow him on the road. Surprisingly, Jesus tells them to go home and tell others what has been done to them. He desires their new relationship, and the conversation that created it, to spread. The woman at the well ran home!

The Practice of Spiritual Conversation

1. Be slow to speak. Be considerate and kind on matters discussed.

    Be slow to speak. Be considerate and kind, especially when it comes to deciding on matters under discussion, or about to be discussed.

2. Listen quietly, and understand. Learn when to speak or be silent.

    Be slow to speak, and speak only after having first listened quietly, so that I may understand the meaning, leanings, and wishes of those who do speak. Thus I will better know when to speak and when to be silent.

3. Be free of attachment to one's own opinion.

    In discussion, I should consider the reasons on both sides without showing any attachment to my own opinion, and try to avoid bringing dissatisfaction to anyone.

4. Do not cite authorities. Deal with everyone equally.

    I should not cite anyone as supporting my opinion . . . and I should deal with everyone on an equal basis, never taking sides with anyone.

5. Speak with humility and sincerity.

    If I ought not to be silent; then I should give my opinion with the greatest possible humility and sincerity, and always end with the words "with due respect for a better opinion."

6. Don't worry about time.

    If I have something to say, it will be of great help to forget about my own leisure or lack of time—that is, my own convenience. I should rather accommodate myself to the convenience of the one with whom I am to deal so that I may influence him (or her) to God's greater glory.

7. Adapt to others.

    Consider their temperaments and adapt to them. If they are of a lively temper, quick and cheerful in speech, follow their lead while speaking to them of good and holy things, and do not be serious, glum, and reserved. If they are shy and retiring, slow to speak, serious, and weighty in their words, use the same manner with them, because such ways will be pleasing to them.

8. Ask the Spirit to descend with abundant gifts.

    Pray and lead others to pray particularly to God our Lord . . . to deign to send forth his Holy Spirit on all who take part in the discussions, so that the Holy Spirit may descend in greater abundance with his grace and gifts (upon the conversations).

9. Awaken knowledge and love.

    Awaken in souls a thorough knowledge of themselves and a love of their Creator and Lord.

10. Open people to God's grace.

    It will be helpful to lead people, as far as possible, to open themselves to God's grace, exhorting them to a desire for salvation, to prayer, to alms and to everything that conduces to receiving grace or increasing it. This will be effected by good example, by friendly contact through the Exercises and by spiritual conversation.

In 1546 Ignatius wrote instructions for three men he was sending to the Council of Trent, the church's great meeting to respond to the Reformation, as theological advisors (Letter 123).[10] The ten notes in "The Practice of Spiritual Conversation" above are from this letter. The drift of Ignatius is clear. Most of his points are countercultural and astonishing for men sent as expert advisors. Then, as today, few people are slow to speak. Three foci are worth highlighting for your receiver.

The first is slowness. Ignatius says, "Be slow to speak," to begin with quiet listening for meaning, for understanding, and above all, for catching the driving desires underneath the other's words. Only then does your receiver make a choice, whether to speak or be silent.

The second focus is freedom. He asks conversing people to be free of personal opinion, quick decisions, attachments, outside authorities, and rigidness. Rather, your receiver should cultivate kindness, compassion, humility, sincerity, and equality, and adapt to the other in her or his manner.

The third focus is openness. Ignatius believes spiritual conversations awaken self-knowledge and love in people, bringing their interior life into the sunshine and enlarging their vision of what could be. They open people up to God's action. In such openness your receiver needs to respect how other receivers express their prayer experience, tell their life story, and communicate need or vulnerability. Group awareness and care in this openness is everyone's responsibility because God is equally in all.

In conversation, your receiver may receive the gift of affectionate awe and loving reverence for the other. Ignatius had a vivid way of encouraging this. He says that those conversing "should proceed from the outward person and look upon creature, not as good looking or attractive, but as someone bathed in the blood of Christ, an image of God, a temple of the Holy Spirit" (Letter 24).[11]

To teach your receiver or group of receivers spiritual conversation, go slowly through "The Practice of Spiritual Conversation" list (pp. 54–55), with examples from both your lives. The guide "Seven Approaches to Spiritual Conversation" (pp. 68–69) could be given to your receiver well into the retreat, for greater depth in daily-life spiritual conversation.

Ask your receiver's to practice sacred conversation with family and friends, at work, etc. In this, each could follow Ignatius in his instructions on paying attention to the person's character and feelings. "As to the manner of doing this, remember that, adapting yourselves to the character and inclinations of persons, you should act with prudence (discretion) and proportion (adaptability)" (Letter 18).[12] Invite your receiver to go gently and with great suppleness.

Prayer before a Spiritual Conversation

Lord give me the time I need for this conversation.
Help me to let go of my own convenience and work
to be fully present to each person here.

May I be slow to speak. Give me the wisdom to listen quietly,
to sense the meaning, positions and desires of each speaker,
to know whether to be silent or speak.

Free me to listen without prejudice, to treat each speaker equally.
Keep me considerate and kind with matters that arise,
sincere in my opinion, respecting better opinions.

Help me to hold each speaker's prayer experience reverently,
their talents and faith gently,
and to enkindle in them love of our Creator and Lord,
and to serve them in body as well as in word.

Let the Spirit descend upon this circle
with an abundance of her gifts.
Above all, give me the greatest possible reverence and humility,
and even affectionate awe,
of the way you dwell in the speakers before me. Amen.

Phase Three: Discernment of Spirits

Ignatius has this advice for you, the giver: "In the matter of desolations and the tricks of the enemy, as well as in the matter of consolations, instructions can be given about the rules for recognizing various spirits" (*Spiritual Exercises* 7). These instructions he calls "the rules by which to perceive and understand to some extent the various movements produced in the soul: the good that they may be accepted, and the bad, that they may be rejected" (*Spiritual Exercises* 313).

Teach these guidelines in mini-discernments so that your receiver may learn to recognize those feelings characteristic of the good and bad spirit. Then invite him or her to purposely accept the good spirit and reject the bad spirit (*Spiritual Exercises* 313). As taught by Jesus, your receiver learns to identify the weeds in the wheat, but stay focused on reaping the harvest (Mt 13:24–30).

In the same regard, Ignatius suggests that you may have to encourage your receiver when he or she is in desolation. "If the giver of the Exercises sees that the exercitant is desolate and tempted, it is important not to be hard or curt with such a person but gentle and kind, to give courage and strength for the future, to lay bare the tricks of the enemy of human nature" (*Spiritual Exercises* 8).

The four discernment guidelines below will help you and your receiver to test everything, and hold fast to what is good (see 1 Thess 5:16–22). Instructions are given in four mini-discernments. They are called mini-discernments because they can be made simply and shortly, in three to seven minutes, after a spiritual exercise or spiritual conversation, or at the end of a day. You will need to go through the sections in italic in the four guidelines, to teach your receiver how they are used in making the mini-discernments. Then you both learn with practice.

The Practice of Discernment of Spirits

Guideline 1. Moving from bad to worse. With people who go from one deadly sin to another, it is the usual practice of the enemy to hold out apparent pleasures, so that he makes them imagine sensual delights and satisfactions in order to maintain and reinforce them in their vices and sins.

With people of this kind, the good spirit uses the opposite procedure, causing pricks of conscience and feelings of remorse by means of the natural power of rational moral judgment.

Guideline 2. Moving from good to better. In the case of people who are making serious progress in the purification of their sins, and who advance from good to better in the service of God our Lord, the procedure is the contrary to that described in guideline one, for then *it is characteristic of the bad spirit to harass, sadden and obstruct, and to disturb with false reasoning, so as to impede progress, while the characteristic of the good spirit is to give courage and strength, consolations, tears, inspirations and quiet, making things easy and removing all obstacles so that the person may move forward in doing good.*

Guideline 3. On spiritual consolation. I use the word *"consolation"* when any interior movement is produced in the soul which leads her to become *inflamed with the love of her Creator* and Lord, and when as a consequence, there is no creature on the face of the earth that the person can love in itself, but he or she loves it in the Creator and Lord of all things.

Similarly, I use the word "consolation" when a person sheds tears which lead to the love of our Lord, whether these arise from grief over sins, or over the passion of Christ our Lord, or because of other reasons immediately directed toward his service and praise.

Lastly, I give the name *"consolation" to every increase of hope, faith and charity, to all interior happiness which calls and attracts to heavenly things and to the salvation of one's soul, leaving the soul quiet and at peace in her Creator and Lord.*

Guideline 4. On spiritual desolation. "Desolation" is the name I give to everything contrary to what is described in guideline three; for example, *darkness and disturbance in the soul, attraction to what is low and of the earth, disquiet arising from various agitations and temptations. All this leads to a lack of confidence in which one feels oneself to be without hope and without love. One finds oneself thoroughly lazy, lukewarm, sad, and as though cut off from one's Creator and Lord.*

For just as consolation is contrary to desolation, in the same way, the thoughts that spring from consolation are contrary to the thoughts that spring from desolation (*Spiritual Exercises* 314–17).

In the beginning it will be enough to just try the first mini-discernment below and, in later weeks of the retreat, to try the others, one by one, until your receiver is confident enough to identify the discernments that matter the most in his or her prayer.

The first two mini-discernments are made referring to the descriptive lists of feelings and consolations that are in italic in the four guidelines of Ignatius above. Your receiver may also experience similar feelings, not listed, that are also filled with the good spirit.

Mini-Discernment 1	**Feelings and spirits**
	What feelings in my prayer are characteristic of the good spirit? These I accept. What are characteristic of the bad spirit? These I reject.

Mini-Discernment 2	**Consolations and desolations**
	Did I experience interior happiness, quiet, love, or spiritual consolations? Did I experience contrary disturbances in desolation?

Mini-Discernment 3	**Good spirit over time**
	Can I see the movement of the good spirit over several exercises or longer? In what direction am I drawn? Can I see the contrary movement of the bad spirit?

Mini-Discernment 4	**Good spirit through others**
	Has my Listening Book revealed deeper desires of the good spirit for me? In my sacred listening, did I also hear the voice of the good spirit? After my spiritual conversations, do I see the life-giving patterns of the good spirit?

Prayer to the Good Spirit

Good Spirit, inflame me with love of my Creator and Lord.

Help me to recognize you in the discernment of spirits,

to find you in the flowing of my courage and strength,

to source you in my consolations, in my tears,

and join you in your inspirations and quiet.

Open my eyes to the disturbance of the bad spirit,

to the sadness and disquiet.

Reveal the darkness of desolation for what it is,

and turn me in the contrary direction.

Please, make things easy for me,

remove all the obstacles in my life

so that I may move forward in doing good.

Direct me toward your service and praise,

increase in me your gifts of hope, faith and love,

fill me with that interior happiness

which calls and attracts to spiritual things,

and leaves my soul quiet

and at peace in her Creator and Lord. Amen.

Advanced Guidelines for the Practice of Discernment of Spirits

These advanced guidelines are for you alone (*Spiritual Exercises* 318–327). You only offer one of these guidelines to your receiver if she or he has already experienced it in prayer or reflection. Then they will be of great help, but not before.

Guidelines five to nine are useful for one caught in spiritual desolation, ten and eleven for times of spiritual consolation. In guidelines twelve to fourteen, Ignatius reveals the behavior of the enemy of our nature, or bad spirit, and how to respond.

Ignatius is a man of his time and culture, with attendant views of men and women. Guidelines twelve and thirteen could well attract the label of sexism. Ignatius himself had deep, respectful and important relationships with women. These two guidelines are kept in this Manual because, putting aside the labels of "woman" and "man," the spiteful and deceitful behavior represented is realistic enough of any person, and thus of the "enemy" who is the subject of the guide.

Acting with courage in the face of the enemy and bringing an unhealthy relationship into the open is still good advice. So is strengthening or protecting a weak spot in personal defenses. As Ignatius often advises, encourage your receiver not only to protect her- or himself, but also to stand up to, expose, and defeat the enemy completely.

In Times of Desolation

Guideline 5. In time of desolation, one should never make any change but should stand firm and constant in the resolutions and decisions by which one was guided the day before the desolation or during the preceding time of consolation. For just as in consolation it is more the good spirit who guides and counsels us, so in desolation it is the bad spirit, and by following his counsels we can never find the right way forward (*Spiritual Exercises* 318).

Guideline 6. Although in desolation we must make no changes in our former decisions, it is nevertheless very profitable to attempt vigorously to make changes in ourselves against this desolation, for example, by more insistence on prayer and meditation, by much examination, and by doing penance in some suitable way (*Spiritual Exercises* 319).

Guideline 7. A person in desolation should consider how our Lord has placed them in a trial period, so that they are to resist the various disturbances and temptations of the enemy by their own natural powers. For this they can do with the divine help which remains with them at all times even though they may not clearly perceive it; although the Lord has withdrawn their fervor, deeply felt love, and intense grace, he has still left them the grace sufficient for eternal salvation (*Spiritual Exercises* 320).

Guideline 8. A person in desolation should work to remain in patience, for patience is opposed to the annoyances which come upon them; and they should keep in mind that consolation will not be long in coming, if they make use of all their powers against this desolation, as has been explained in guideline six (*Spiritual Exercises* 321).

Guideline 9. There are three principal causes for our finding ourselves in desolation. The first is that we are lukewarm, lazy, or careless in the practices of the spiritual life; so spiritual consolation goes away because of our faults.

Secondly, spiritual desolation tests our quality and shows how far we will extend ourselves in God's service and praise without the generous remuneration of consolations and overflowing graces.

Thirdly, spiritual desolation gives us true knowledge and understanding, so that we may perceive within ourselves that on our part we cannot arouse or sustain overflowing devotion, intense love, tears, or any other spiritual consolation, but that all this is a gift and grace from God our Lord. So we are not to build our nest where we do not belong, becoming elated in mind to the point of pride and vainglory, and putting down to our own account devotion or other forms of spiritual consolation (*Spiritual Exercises* 322).

In Times of Consolation

Guideline 10. A person in consolation should think how they shall bear themselves in the desolation which will follow later, and gather renewed strength for that moment (*Spiritual Exercises* 323).

Guideline 11. Persons in consolation should try to humble and lower themselves as much as possible by thinking how little they are worth in time of desolation without this grace of consolation. On the other hand, the person in desolation should keep in mind that they can do much if they draw strength from their Creator and Lord, having the grace sufficient to resist every enemy (*Spiritual Exercises* 324).

How the Enemy Behaves

Guideline 12. The behavior of the enemy resembles that of a woman in a quarrel with a man, for he is weak when faced with strength but strong when faced with weakness. It is characteristic of a woman when she quarrels with a man to lose heart and to take flight when the man shows a bold front; on the other hand, the moment the man gives way and loses courage, then the rage, vengeance, and ferocity of the woman overflow and know no bounds.

In the same way, it is characteristic of the enemy to weaken and lose courage and to turn to flight with his temptations, when the person engaged in the spiritual life shows a bold front against those temptations and acts in a way diametrically opposed to them. If, on the contrary, such a person begins to be afraid and to lose courage in sustaining temptation, no wild beast on the face of the earth is as ferocious as the enemy of human nature in the surging malice with which he pursues his wicked purpose (*Spiritual Exercises* 325).

Guideline 13. The enemy also behaves as a false lover behaves toward a woman. Such a man wants to remain hidden and not to be discovered. In using dishonest talk to try to seduce the daughter of a good father, or the wife of a good husband, he wants his words and inducements kept secret. On the other hand, when the daughter reveals his smooth words and corrupt intentions to her father (or the wife to her husband), he is very much put out, for he then easily recognizes that his plans cannot succeed.

In the same way, when the enemy of human nature brings his deceits and inducements to bear on the just soul, he wants them to be received and kept in secret. When they are revealed to a good confessor or some other person who knows his trickery and perversity, he is very displeased, realizing that once his tricks are revealed his malicious purpose cannot succeed (*Spiritual Exercises* 326).

Guideline 14. Likewise, he behaves like a military leader, setting about the conquest and seizure of the object he desires. The commander of an army, after setting up his camp and inspecting the fortifications and defenses of a fortress, attacks it at its weakest point. In the same way, the enemy of our human nature makes his rounds to inspect all our virtues, theological, cardinal, and moral, and where he finds us weakest and in greatest need as regards our eternal salvation, there he attacks and tries to take us (*Spiritual Exercises* 327).

Seven Approaches to Spiritual Conversation

Ignatius, in his own words, for wiser spiritual conversations in daily life.

1. Assume good in the other's statement and viewpoint.

   So that the giver of the Exercises and the exercitant (receiver) may the better help and benefit each other, it must be presupposed that every good Christian should be readier to justify than to condemn a neighbor's statement. If no justification can be found, one should ask the other in what sense the statement is to be taken, and if that sense is wrong the other should be corrected with love (*Spiritual Exercises* 22).

2. Begin at the bottom and adapt.

   He should preserve the proper manner of proceeding, aiming at humility by starting from below and not getting involved in higher matters except when invited or asked, unless discretion should dictate otherwise, taking into consideration time, place, and persons. This discretion cannot be confined within any rule. The manner also includes working to obtain the goodwill of the persons with whom he deals, by a manifestation grounded in (showing in himself) truth, virtue and love . . . and adapting himself to all with holy prudence (Letter 24).[13]

3. Go in the other person's door.

   Acting for good, we can praise a person or go along with him on some particular good point, passing over in silence any bad points he may have. Once we have won his love, we will better get what we want (success in inviting the person to greater service of God). Thus we go in his door and come out our own (Letter 32).

4. Develop interior composure and maturity.

   This will be much fostered by outward as well as inward gravity in your gait (walking) and gestures, the propriety of your dress, and especially the circumspection of your speech and the maturity of your counsel on both practical and doctrinal maters. This maturity entails not hastily giving your opinion on any question (unless it is quite easy), but taking time to think about it, study it, or consult with others (Letter 18; Appendix 1, pp. 239–47).

5. Listen long and willingly.

    In dealings with anyone, say little and be slow to speak. Listen long
    and willingly, until they have finished what they wanted to say. Then
    reply, point by point, come to an end, and take your leave. If the per-
    son rejoins, cut the rejoinders as short as possible; your leave-taking
    should be swift and gracious (Letter 32).

6. Remain in the middle way.

    You should make yourselves beloved by your humility and char-
    ity, becoming all things to all men. Where factions and part strife
    prevail, you should not take a stand against either side, but instead
    show that you remain in the middle and love both parties (Letter
    18).[14]

7. Speak with order, kindness, and love when urging spiritual progress.

    In discussion be slow to speak and speak little. But if you wish to
    urge souls to make progress in the spiritual life, it will be better to
    speak at length, with order, and with kindness and love (Letter 123).

PART THREE

A GIVER OF

THE FIRST
Spiritual
EXERCISES

STRUCTURE AND DYNAMIC OF THE FIRST SPIRITUAL EXERCISES

The Structure and Dynamic of the FSE Retreats

The FSE retreats are given for twenty-one to twenty-five days in daily life. Prayer, in the form of a spiritual exercise, is made four days a week, over four weeks. A weekend exercise and Sunday Eucharist are also included. Each prayer day has a spiritual exercise and Listening Book reflection.

Each FSE retreat is structured to be experienced as a whole, with a dynamic that moves through all four weeks. When the integrity of the whole is broken, the big picture and connections are lost. The full four weeks gives serious time to God.

In a similar way, each week has its own dynamic. Using the daily exercises, your receiver is guided through certain larger movements. A week has its own integrity, and made in order, serves the desire for the primary gift and inner peace in each FSE retreat.

The exercise prayer texts are carefully chosen as both single texts and a network of texts. As single texts, they provide the context, relationships and content of each spiritual exercise. Incidentally, they shed light on core elements of Christian faith.

As a network of texts, each text gives and receives life from the others. They offer each other different views, contrast of content, and masculine and feminine experience. Personal meanings will emerge each week as the Spirit takes your receiver forward.

Each FSE retreat deliberately introduces many different images of God in action. In this way, a variety of divine relationships may give your receiver an experience of the extraordinary richness of knowing and loving God, of being loved by the Trinity.

The Structure and Dynamic of an FSE Exercise

Preparation	I consider where I am going and why.
	I make a gesture of reverence and humility.
	I read the prayer texts.
Opening Prayer	I ask for the grace to direct my whole self to God.
Desire	I desire . . .
Prayer	Using my imagination, I . . .
Conversation	I end my prayer in a short conversation with God, talking as to a friend, about what I have just experienced. Our Father.

The Ignatian spiritual exercise is a structured, guided, and shaped prayer. It is structured by five steps. It is guided by the Prayer in step four and the prayer texts. It is shaped by the given desire, the life experience of your receiver and God's response to both. Ignatius insisted on all five points. Why? The answer is in their depth and relationship to one another (*Spiritual Exercises* 46–48, 54, 75–76).

The *Preparation* is for focus and sacred space. Your receiver takes an inner journey from an ordinary place to a holy place. Ignatius asks your receiver to consider where she or he is going and why. This preparation can be a potent union of reverence, body, sacred space, and imagination.

The *Opening Prayer* is about the surrender of self. Offering all intentions and actions, it is a personal response to the felt presence of God in the Preparation. It is a mini-*contemplatio*, where lovers give and receive from each other. Ignatius adds service and praise in his longer prayer, "I ask God our Lord for grace that all my intentions, actions and operations may be directed purely to the service and praise of his Divine Majesty" (*Spiritual Exercises* 46, 49).

The *Desire* gives the exercise its purpose. It is essential. Your receiver directs his or her desire to God, just as Jesus instructs, to ask, knock, and search. And like Jesus, Ignatius asks your receiver to stay with this desire until it is answered.

The *Prayer* is the structure that brings your receiver fully into relationship with God. It is where she or he enters into a gospel scene, meditates, or takes the steps through a consideration.

The *Conversation* is a spiritual conversation between your receiver and God. It is a time to talk about feelings arising from prayer, to receive help, advice, and encouragement as with a friend. The Our Father returns your receiver to the ordinary place, daily life, to the stance of "thy kingdom come."

Each step is a prayer in itself. But received together, in order, they create a powerful dynamic for your receiver: from offering to desire and receiving, from solitude to intimacy and friendship with God, from grace to gratitude and helping others. This is why Ignatius insists on the full five steps.

The Structure and Dynamic of Spiritual Conversation

The structure and dynamic of spiritual conversation is fully explained in Part Two of this Manual. Here the dynamic of spiritual conversation is considered. This structure of creating this dynamic is:

Contemplative Silence	Listen to the loving Trinity.
1. Listening	Listen to new things received in prayer.
2. Conversation	Conversation on prayer experiences.
3. Discernment	Listen to mini-discernments of the spirits.
Contemplative Silence	Listen to the active Trinity.

Each week, your receiver is learning a new prayer method, engaging deeply with personal desires and memories, responding to God, praying new exercises each day, and integrating all this into his or her life. Often anxieties arise about how things are going when in fact she or he is doing well. Graces abound and await the opportunity to be named and shared with others.

So offering a spiritual conversation once a weekend for the four weeks of a retreat is essential. If you have a group, you might also offer individuals a personal spiritual conversation, if needed or desired, outside of the weekly group conversations.

In the dynamic of the FSE, spiritual conversation is as important as the spiritual exercise. Each discloses new meaning in the other. Each "re-members" the other into greater wholeness. Each nurtures the grace and desire of the exercise, and brings them to birth. Each is drawn to greater life through sharing with wider and wider groups. This is the double helix of prayer and spiritual conversation.

GIVING
INNER PEACE IN
DIVINE LOVE

Clothe

yourselves with love,

which binds everything together

in perfect harmony.

And let the peace of Christ

rule in your hearts,

to which indeed you were called in the one body.

And be thankful.

Let the word of Christ dwell in you richly.

And whatever you do,

in word or deed,

do everything in the name of the Lord Jesus,

giving thanks to God the Father

through him.

—Colossians 3:14–17

1. The Purpose of This Retreat

The primary purpose of this retreat is to remember, experience, and express love. In the words of Ignatius, "to desire an interior knowledge of all the good I have received, so that acknowledging this with gratitude, I may be able to love and serve his Divine Majesty in everything" (*Spiritual Exercises* 233). This desire is found in the exercise titled the Contemplation to Receive Divine Love, or *Contemplatio*. This retreat is built around the *Contemplatio*, drawing it out from a single-day exercise to a spacious four weeks of exercises.

Ignatius begins the *Contemplatio* with a note that love consists in mutual communication. He continues, "The lover gives and communicates to the loved one what they have, or something of what they have, or are able to give; and in turn the one loved does the same for the lover. Each gives to the other" (*Spiritual Exercises* 231). This receiving and giving relationship is at the heart of the retreat, considered in your receiver's experience of love, in intimacy with the Trinity, and in the gifts of a loving God.

Your receiver, having considered all the gifts of love flowing to her or him, is invited to respond. In the beginning of the *Contemplatio*, Ignatius notes, "It will be good to notice that love ought to find its expression in deeds rather than in words" (*Spiritual Exercises* 230). Here then, with renewed awareness and gratitude, is the practical purpose of this retreat.

Retreat Map

The retreat map offers a way to see the structure of the retreat. It shows week titles which reveal the focus of each week. The daily titles reveal how one day's content is connected to the next and ultimately reveals the path taken to experience the love of God. A retreat map is a good way to understand the purpose of a retreat.

WEEK ONE	REMEMBERING LOVE
Monday	I remember being loved.
Tuesday	I remember being loved and grateful.
Wednesday	I remember being loved and responding.
Thursday	I remember a loving friendship.
Sunday	Action in memory of love

WEEK TWO	DWELLING IN LOVE
Monday	I abide in the love of Jesus.
Tuesday	I dwell in the love of the Father.
Wednesday	I remain in the love of the Spirit.
Thursday	Inseparable from God's love
Sunday	Action in union with love

WEEK THREE	LOVE AT WORK
Monday	I remember the gifts I have received.
Tuesday	I see how God dwells in creation.
Wednesday	I see how God dwells in me.
Thursday	I see how God works in creation and me.
Saturday	Reconciliation Examen
Sunday	Action in gratitude of love

WEEK FOUR	LOVE IN SERVICE
Monday	Every gift descends like the sun's rays.
Tuesday	Every gift flows like water.
Wednesday	Give me only the grace to love you.
Thursday	Awareness Examen
Saturday	Program for Life
Sunday	Action in peace with love

Desires Map

Each day your receiver takes the given desire of an exercise in trust and surrender. Each day God communicates personally with your receiver. The desires map allows you to chart this flow of desires and keep your receiver focused. Comparing all four retreat and desire maps is useful to consider the suitability of each retreat for someone.

WEEK ONE	REMEMBERING LOVE
Monday	I desire to feel the love in my life.
Tuesday	I desire to feel loved and grateful.
Wednesday	I desire to feel the love and my response.
Thursday	I desire to feel a loving friendship.
Sunday	I desire to act in the memory of love.

WEEK TWO	DWELLING IN LOVE
Monday	I desire to abide in the love of Jesus.
Tuesday	I desire to dwell in the love of the Father.
Wednesday	I desire to remain in the love of the Spirit.
Thursday	I desire the inseparable love of the Trinity.
Sunday	I desire to act in union with love.

WEEK THREE	LOVE AT WORK
Monday	I desire to ponder the gifts I have received.
Tuesday	I desire to ponder how God dwells in creation.
Wednesday	I desire to ponder how God dwells in me.
Thursday	I desire to ponder how God works in creation and me.
Sunday	I desire to act in gratitude of love.

WEEK FOUR	LOVE IN SERVICE
Monday	I desire to see how every gift from God to me descends like a sun ray.
Tuesday	I desire to see how every gift flows like water.
Wednesday	I desire only the grace to love my God.
Saturday	I desire to create a Program for Life.
Sunday	I desire to act in peace with love.

2. Content and Dynamic

WEEK ONE	REMEMBERING LOVE	
Monday	I remember being loved.	
Tuesday	I remember being loved and grateful.	
Wednesday	I remember being loved and responding.	
Thursday	I remember a loving friendship.	
Sunday	Action in memory of love.	Eucharist

Everyone carries the memory of good things. In the first week you take your receiver back into her or his past to remember their experiences of being loved, and how it felt at that time. Then the exercise takes those feelings into the present. This is the dynamic of the week.

The basic movement in each exercise is from then to now and now to then. It is a cycle that becomes clear and powerful with repetition. Feelings of love become built up in the now. This is the content. It charges the prayer. It is a week of strong memories, feelings and often tears.

The only progression through the week is adding gratitude and response to the experience of being loved. And because friendship with Jesus is a prime relationship in the FSE, the fourth-day exercise remembers loving friendship. Before week's end, you may show or confirm with your receiver this key truth: the feelings of "being loved" now are real feelings not memories.

WEEK TWO	DWELLING IN LOVE	
Monday	I abide in the love of Jesus.	
Tuesday	I dwell in the love of the Father.	
Wednesday	I remain in the love of the Spirit.	
Thursday	Inseparable from God's love.	
Sunday	Action in union with love.	Eucharist

This is a quiet and contemplative week. The content is the invitations from each person of the Trinity to your receiver. The week is founded on one great desire of Jesus, "As the Father has loved me, so I have loved you; abide in my love. I have said these things to you so that my joy may be in you, and that your joy may be complete" (Jn 15:9,11–15). The Greek verb "to abide" may be translated to "live in" or "dwell in" or "remain in." It describes a deep union, one that is life-giving and fruitful.

In each exercise, your receiver is given similar texts, words of the heart, addressed to her or him. The first part of the dynamic then is deep listening and response to the words repeated by Jesus each day in the upper room. Your receiver needs to find him- or herself there.

The second part of the dynamic is accepting those invitations and abiding in the love of God. Here is stillness and quiet, union and joy. Here your receiver may express one or all of the three desiring prayers. It is not that your receiver already has these feelings, but rather that they are desired. Your receiver may have the awkwardness of hearing or saying "I love you" for the first time.

WEEK THREE	LOVE AT WORK	
Monday	I remember the gifts I have received.	
Tuesday	I see how God dwells in creation.	
Wednesday	I see how God dwells in me.	
Thursday	I see how God works in creation and me.	
Saturday	Reconciliation Examen	
Sunday	Action in gratitude of love.	Eucharist

This week you give the first half of the *Contemplatio* exercise. The dynamic is for your receiver to remember all the good things she or he has received from the Creator and Lord. With the remembering comes the awareness of how they are given with such love. Then, feeling gratitude your receiver responds with his or her offering and desired action. If the first half of this retreat is about remembering and feeling love, the second half is about love in action. The exercise is the same for each day, with only the content of point one and point three being changed.

The four exercises take a point each from the *Contemplatio*, exactly as written by Ignatius. He drives the dynamic here; the gifts move from personal ones to Jesus himself. The self-giving God moves from "dwelling in" to "working in" your receiver and all creation.

WEEK FOUR	LOVE IN SERVICE
Monday	Every gift descends like the sun's rays.
Tuesday	Every gift flows like water.
Wednesday	Give me only the grace to love you.
Thursday	Awareness Examen
Saturday	Program for Life

Sunday   Action in peace with love. Eucharist

This week the second half of the *Contemplatio* exercise is made with the same five-point structure used last week. The content continues from last week, with only points one and three being different.

The dynamic of the week is about streaming sun rays and water, the flow of gifts from God to your receiver, and the flow back of your receiver's whole self, and all his or her gifts, to God. The focus is clearly love and gift, but set in the large and generous scale of the whole of the universe.

The last spiritual exercise, Eucharist, and Program for Life complete this retreat with love in action. You give your receiver the Program for Life for choosing realistic choices to love and help others.

The Awareness Examen's five-point structure is deliberately used to structure the points of the *Contemplatio*. This works well, both because your receiver gets to take the Awareness Examen home after having prayed its essential movement for two weeks, and because the Awareness Examen is a daily *Contemplatio*, an exercise to find God's love at work in your receiver's day.

3. New Prayer Methods

The new prayer methods are those exercise methods that are new to your receiver. You will need to learn and practice them until you are confident to give them.

New Prayer Method 1: I remember being loved.

Preparation	I take a relaxed position with a straight back, my body poised for prayer.
	I make a gesture of reverence and humility.
	I read the prayer text about passionate love.
Opening Prayer	I ask for the grace to direct my whole self toward God.
Desire	I desire to feel the love in my life.
Prayer	Using my imagination, I remember an experience of being really loved.
	I go back in time to re-create this experience as best I can with the details of place, weather, conversation, actions, and people. I relive the experience with all my senses—I touch, smell, hear, and feel being so loved.
	I remain in this place for a few minutes.
	Now, eyes still closed, I come back into the room where I am now. I remember the details of place here. How do I feel? I remain here for a few minutes.
	I return again to the place where I was loved, I relive being loved. Do I feel any different than the first time I came here? I remain for a few minutes.
	I come back into the room where I am now. How do I feel? Different? Now I move back and forth between both places, spending a minute or so in each.
	I note any change of feelings. I do this for five minutes.
Conversation	I end my prayer in a short conversation with God, talking as to a friend, about what I have just experienced. Our Father.

Suggested Prayer Time: 25 minutes

Preparation: 5 minutes. Opening Prayer: 1 minute. Desire: 1 minute. Prayer: 15 minutes. Conversation: 3 minutes. Listening Book after prayer: 10 minutes.

How to Give This Exercise

The title of this exercise is "I remember being loved." It is day one, Monday of Week One of this retreat. The prayer method is the same each day this week. To actually give the exercises of any FSE retreat, simply read the text of the exercise, pausing at the appropriate places. The five-point structure, excepting the examens, is virtually the same for every FSE exercise. You also read one or several prayer texts where indicated.

You need to be aware that when some receivers do this exercise, the opposite memory springs into their minds, the loss or lack of being loved. So after accepting this in your receiver's life, ask her or him to just take the "being loved" part of the experience. Anything else will drag her or him away from the desired grace and bring the painful feelings into the present. Your job is to gently encourage back to the joyful.

Each day your receiver may choose the same or a different experience of being loved. Know that nearly all receivers who find this exercise hard do find their way by week's end. This exercise can also be usefully made for shorter times. The most important repeating question is, "How do I feel here and now?" Always leave time for the answer to settle in your receiver's heart.

New Prayer Method 2: I abide in the love of Jesus.

Preparation	I take a relaxed position with a straight back, my body poised for prayer.
	I make a gesture of reverence and humility.
Opening Prayer	I ask for the grace to direct my whole self toward Jesus.
Desire	I desire to abide in the love of Jesus.
Prayer	I use my imagination to re-create the scene of the Last Supper with the details of place, conversation, actions and people. Then I take my place at the table.
	I hear Jesus address me personally. Slowly reading the prayer text, I listen to his joyful words, each singing in my heart.
	In response, I abide in Jesus while saying to him, gently and often, each desiring statement below for a few minutes each:
	"I abide in your love."
	"I am enjoyed by you."
	"I feel complete in you."
Conversation	I end my prayer with the Our Father.

Suggested Prayer Time: 25 minutes

Preparation and Opening Prayer: 2 minutes. Desire: 1 minute. Prayer: 20 minutes. Conversation: 2 minutes. Listening Book after prayer: 10 minutes.

How to Give This Exercise

The title of this exercise is "I abide in the love of Jesus." It is day six, Monday of Week Two of this retreat. Again you will need to guide your receiver through this new exercise, to give her or him an example of the timing and pace of it. Afterward, give your receiver time for questions to you based on her or his actual experience of it.

The first part of the prayer uses imaginative contemplation which is likely new to your receiver. Guide your receiver and let him or her find their way. Most receivers, after practice, find it comes to them and they suddenly feel in the real presence of Jesus.

In the second half, you need to be aware that your receiver may not have prayed in contemplative prayer. He or she can sometimes feel as if nothing is happening. It will be helpful to gently encourage your receiver, reminding him or her that once one has come into the presence of God and expressed one's desire, whatever follows in that silent presence is prayer.

Distractions are also likely in this prayer. Teach your receiver that all he or she needs to do is repeat one of the three desiring prayers, such as "I remain in you." This will bring her or him back into relationship with God and thus prayer. Practicing this exercise at home or with a group you are already a part of and talking about it will help you immensely in giving it to your receiver.

New Prayer Method 3: I remember the gifts I have received.

Be Loved	After slowly reading the prayer texts, I stand for a few minutes, precious in God's sight, and honored. I allow God's compassion to wash through me.
Ask Help	I ask the Spirit for an interior knowledge of all the good I have received.
Remember	I ponder with deep affection how God is loving me:
	I remember the benefits I have received: creation, redemption, and personal gifts.
	I review how much God has done for me, how much I have been given of what belongs to God.
	I reflect on how the Father, Son and Spirit even wish to give me themselves.
Response	I respond to God as a friend, beautiful creature, or lover.
	With the Communion of Saints in support, I express my gratitude.
Offering	I consider what, in all reason and justice, I ought to offer and give God. I conclude, saying, as one making a gift with heartfelt love:
	Take Lord and receive, all my liberty, my memory, my understanding, and my entire will, all that I have and possess. You gave it all to me; to you I return it. All is yours, dispose of it entirely according to your will. Give me only the grace to love you, for that is enough for me.

Suggested Prayer Time: 40 minutes

Be Loved: 10 minutes. Ask Help: 1 minute. Remember: 20 minutes. Response: 4 minutes. Offering: 5 minutes. Listening Book after prayer: 10 minutes.

How to Give This Exercise

The title of this exercise is "I remember the gifts I have received." It is day eleven, Monday of Week Three of this retreat, and the last new prayer method of the retreat. The five-point structure is new and is based on the five points of the Awareness Examen. This is deliberate, as explained above in the content and dynamic of the fourth week.

The Awareness and Reconciliation Examens, also made in the last two weeks, are new prayer methods themselves and "common to all retreats." You will find advice on how to give them in the collection of similar exercises in this Manual (pp. 154–55, 158–59).

The image of relationship with God used in the first "Be Loved" point is usually taken from the first prayer text. The third "remember" point has the greatest content, so you can shorten or lengthen the time spent in this point, according to the time available for prayer. The last two points are the same every day.

Practice in giving this exercise or the Awareness Examen to friends, or willing strangers, will increase your confidence to give them to your receiver.

4. Images of God in Action

An FSE retreat deliberately includes many images of God. Most exercises also feature particular actions of each person in the Trinity. These may be found in every part of an exercise, and linked together they can make a series over a week or longer.

In this retreat there are three such series: the faces of love, the voices of love, and the relationships of love. They have a collective or deepening effect over time. Having these sets here at hand may help you, the giver of the FSE, to see what is hidden in a retreat: cumulative images of God in action. But, crucially, you must let your receiver experience them for him- or herself.

The faces of love	In the prayer texts
Week One	Passionate love
	Steadfast love
	Tender love
	Renewing love
	Life-giving love
Week Two	Abiding love
	Intimate love
	Spirit-filled love
	Inseparable love
	Unifying love
Week Three	Compassionate love
	Creative love
	Active love
	Unconditional love
	Gracious love
Week Four	Enlightening love
	Thirst-quenching love
	Humble love
	Just love
	Peaceful love

The voices of love	In the Week Two prayer
Day 1	I abide in your love.
	I am enjoyed by you.
	I feel complete in you.
Day 2	I remain in your love.
	I am at peace in you.
	I feel alive in you.
Day 3	I dwell in your love.
	I am one in you.
	I am at home in you.
Day 4	I am inseparable from your love.
	I love you.
	Thank you.

Loving relationships	In the preparation steps and prayer texts
Week Three	I stand for a few minutes, precious in God's sight, and honored.
	I allow God's compassion to wash through me.
	I stand before the Creator as creature, wonderfully made in God's image.
	I allow God's declaration of my goodness to wash through me.
	I stand for a few minutes and imagine the Spirit living in me, creating a home and sacred place, making me holy.
	I allow God's unconditional love to wash through me.
	I stand for a few minutes before the Trinity, each person giving me life. I imagine them preparing for their work today.
	I allow their desire for working in the world to wash through me.
Week Four	I stand for a few minutes before the Father of lights,
	bathed in the brightness of his generosity.
	I allow his light to wash through me.
	I stand for a few minutes before the Lord of the spring rains.
	I allow Jesus, the living water, to wash through me.

I stand before Jesus and imagine him humbly washing my feet.

I allow the utter fullness of God to wash through me.

GIVING INNER PEACE IN DARKNESS AND LIGHT

God has rescued us

from the power of darkness

and transferred us into the kingdom

of his beloved Son,

in whom we have redemption,

the forgiveness of sins.

In him all the fullness of God

was pleased to dwell,

and through him God was pleased

to reconcile to himself all things,

whether on earth or in heaven,

by making peace

through the blood of his cross.

—Colossians 1:13–20

1. The Purpose of This Retreat

The purpose of this retreat is found in the titles each week. Your receiver is invited to enter progressively into the mysteries of love, mercy, healing and freedom. Or more directly, your receiver seeks unconditional love, forgiveness, healing or freedom from attachments. Usually one of these becomes the focus of desire for your receiver. If so, the other three will give extra meaning to her or his primary desire. The purpose of this retreat is to help your receiver to move forward in life with greater depth.

The lack of love, mercy, healing or true meaning in life can easily be felt as a darkness. *The First Spiritual Exercises* book describes such darkness: "There are many forms of inner darkness—the pervasive gray of disorder in my life, the unrelenting black of living with evil or the results of sinfulness, the bleak nights of chronic illness or suffering, the dark pit of the unfree where attachments imprison me, and the blinding confusion that the bad spirit can wrap around my eyes." So the express purpose of this retreat is to bring light into your receiver's life.

Zechariah, the uncle of Jesus, expresses this purpose well: "By the tender mercy of our God, the dawn from on high will break upon us, to give light to those who sit in darkness and in the shadow of death, to guide our feet into the way of peace" (Lk 1:79).

Through exercises, then, you guide your receiver through this darkness into light and peace. These are not easy journeys, yet they are deeply needed by most people at some time in their lives. This retreat asks your receiver to put her or his net into "deep" water (see Lk 5:1–11). Jesus wishes to fill it with overflowing, liberating, life-giving graces, including himself. This is the purpose of Jesus and thus of this retreat.

Retreat Map

Note how each examen gathers up the movement of the week.

WEEK ONE	THE MYSTERY OF LOVE
Monday	Inner peace
Tuesday	Re-creation
Wednesday	Encouragement
Thursday	Harmony
Saturday	Particular Examen
Sunday	Memory of water

WEEK TWO	THE MYSTERY OF MERCY
Monday	Father at work in the world
Tuesday	Spirit at work in my weakness
Wednesday	Light and darkness
Thursday	Jesus at work in tender love
Saturday	Reconciliation Examen
Sunday	Feast for a celebration

WEEK THREE	THE MYSTERY OF HEALING
Monday	*Ephphatha*! Be opened!
Tuesday	Stand up and walk!
Wednesday	Tormenting demon, come out!
Thursday	*Talitha cum*, rise!
Saturday	Healing Examen
Sunday	Sabbath for setting free

WEEK FOUR	THE MYSTERY OF FREEDOM
Monday	Praise
Tuesday	Reverence
Wednesday	Service
Thursday	Foundation for life
Friday	Program for Life
Saturday	Awareness Examen
Sunday	Being a light of the world

Desires Map

Note how the Sunday exercises express the desires of the week. See also how the last three exercises strongly affirm and support each other.

WEEK ONE — **THE MYSTERY OF LOVE**

Monday	I desire inner peace.
Tuesday	I desire re-creation.
Wednesday	I desire encouragement.
Thursday	I desire harmony.
Sunday	I desire newness of life.

WEEK TWO — **THE MYSTERY OF MERCY**

Monday	I desire the tender mercy of the Father.
Tuesday	I desire intense sorrow for my sins.
Wednesday	I desire intense joy for my life.
Thursday	I desire the tender love of Jesus.
Sunday	I desire to celebrate the mercy of God.

WEEK THREE — **THE MYSTERY OF HEALING**

Monday	I desire to see, hear and speak clearly.
Tuesday	I desire to stand up, move and walk.
Wednesday	I desire to be free of tormenting demons.
Thursday	I desire to be raised back to life.
Sunday	I desire life on the Sabbath.

WEEK FOUR — **THE MYSTERY OF FREEDOM**

Monday	I desire to praise.
Tuesday	I desire to reverence.
Wednesday	I desire to serve.
Thursday	I desire a foundation for my life.
Friday	I desire to create a Program for Life.
Sunday	I desire to be a light in the world.

2. Content and Dynamic

WEEK ONE	THE MYSTERY OF LOVE	
Monday	Inner peace	
Tuesday	Re-creation	
Wednesday	Encouragement	
Thursday	Harmony	
Saturday	Particular Examen	
Sunday	Memory of water	Eucharist

The spiritual exercises of this week are a necessary preparation for the following weeks. Without having experienced the love of a personal God, it will be difficult for your receiver to be open to the graces of the coming weeks. Guilt, self-absorption, or shallow intellectual engagement may block your receiver's acceptance of sinfulness, the need for God's mercy and the freedom to grow.

The dynamic of the week is one of gracious, gentle soaking in the personal love of God. How the receiver will experience this is up to God. The prayer texts and exercises guide the receiver into four places where a personal and intimate relationship with the Trinity may be found.

Throughout this retreat, the receiver prays with two prayer methods, imaginative contemplation and the Particular Examen. The first sharpens your receiver's image of God's action; the second hones her or his desire. The resonance between the longer exercise and the shorter examen can grow into a creative dynamic of personal growth and self-acceptance.

WEEK TWO	THE MYSTERY OF MERCY	
Monday	Father at work in the world	Particular Examen
Tuesday	Spirit at work in my weakness	Particular Examen
Wednesday	Light and Darkness	Particular Examen
Thursday	Jesus at work in tender love	Particular Examen
Saturday	Reconciliation Examen	
Sunday	Feast for a celebration	Eucharist

This week takes your receiver into the deepest movements of Christian life—love and sin, sorrow and wonder, death and life, humility and mercy. The exercises are from the first week of the Full Spiritual Exercises. Calling on a mounting and intense sorrow, they all seek the mercy of God. The

Hebrew word for mercy, *hesed*, is translated with different words in English. It can be kindness, steadfast love or compassion. It can be translated as divine forgiveness or even as a nurturing womb.

Ignatius shapes the dynamic of this week by heightening the dark reality of sin so that the Father's love, through Jesus on the cross, might be experienced as light and life. The content of the exercises is sin outside your receiver, sin inside your receiver, the real consequences of sin, and love for your receiver by Jesus crucified.

But your receiver is already swamped with images of hell on earth in the media. So this week will consider love at work as the first reality, and then sin. The exercises therefore focus on love outside your receiver, love inside your receiver, the real consequences of being loved, and the love of your receiver by Jesus crucified. This then is the fundamental dynamic for the week: that a humble, contrite heart may ask for mercy and receive it. This is the Trinity "at work" in creation, humanity, and your receiver.

WEEK THREE	THE MYSTERY OF HEALING	
Monday	*Ephphatha*! Be opened!	Particular Examen
Tuesday	Stand up and walk!	Particular Examen
Wednesday	Tormenting demon, come out!	Particular Examen
Thursday	*Talitha cum*, rise!	Particular Examen
Saturday	Healing Examen	
Sunday	Sabbath for setting free	Eucharist

The content of this week is the healing events in the gospels. These have been gathered into groups of similar healings, each exercise containing one of these groups. So they cover the healing of the deaf, dumb and blind; the healing of the lame and paralyzed; the healing of those tormented by demons; and the raising of the dead. Sabbath healings are prayed on a Sunday.

The dynamic is simple. Each exercise has three healings of the same group. Your receiver chooses the one that holds the healing most desired. This is likely to be as much metaphorical as actual. So your receiver might ask to be healed of a "blindness" in life or a "paralysis" that is stopping her or him moving forward. Having chosen a healing, your receiver uses imaginative contemplation to enter into the story. This simple dynamic, from lived experience to gospel experience, brings the receiver into relationship with Jesus the healer. What follows is in his hands.

There is dynamic running through the week at another level. Few people ever have the opportunity to enter into the mystery of healing, and of the Healer, by praying each of the different healings over a week. A receiver who desires all the kinds of healing may discover, or be given, a very deep understanding and vision of life—possibly even a call to heal others in some manner.

WEEK FOUR	THE MYSTERY OF FREEDOM	
Monday	Praise	Particular Examen
Tuesday	Reverence	Particular Examen
Wednesday	Service	Particular Examen
Thursday	Foundation for Life	Particular Examen
Friday	Program for Life	
Saturday	Awareness Examen	
Sunday	Being a light of the world	Eucharist

A meditation called the Foundation is the first exercise in the Spiritual Exercises. This week prays the Foundation in detail. The dynamic begins with your receiver getting in touch with her or his experience of praise, reverence and service. The Listening Book is used and discernment made of what is important and worth seeking in each exercise.

After this, your receiver contemplates four versions of the Foundation text and chooses one. With this in hand, the discernment continues on what binds and what frees, what will help your receiver to find balance and indifference in life. Finally, your receiver makes two small, sustainable choices that give his or her life greater freedom and purpose. The dynamic is a cumulative discernment for freedom in future choices.

Note that the first four exercises deliberately use the five-point Awareness Examen structure so that by the end of the week your receiver will have learned the Awareness Examen with unconscious ease. In the final exercise, your receiver creates a Program for Life and learns the Awareness Examen to help him or her become a light to the world.

3. New Prayer Methods

New Prayer Method 1: Inner peace

Preparation	Immediately on waking, I rouse my desire for inner peace by imagining Jesus calming the sea around me. I will get dressed with thoughts like these.
	At my prayer place, I stand, my mind raised up, to consider how God is looking at me with serenity. I make a gesture of reverence and humility.
Opening Prayer	I ask for the grace to direct my whole self toward the Trinity.
Desire	I desire inner peace in the Trinity.
Prayer	I read the prayer texts to understand the power of deep inner peace.
	Using my imagination, I re-create a favorite place where, like Mary, I might sit happily with the Trinity. I imagine the details of place, sounds, smells, etc. Then, as guided below, I hear what each person of the Trinity has to say to me:
	I turn to my Creator. He tells me not to be afraid, that he honors and loves me. I welcome his protection from the fires and floods of my life. I hear his assurance that I will never be abandoned or overwhelmed. Serenity descends upon me.
	I turn to Jesus, who leans forward to tell me nothing shall ever separate me from his love. He takes my fears and troubles in his hands and gives me his peace. Inner peace fills me.
	I turn to the Spirit, the comforter, who invites me to surrender myself to her.
	I rest against the heart of God my Mother. Calm and quiet flow through me.
Conversation	I end in a short conversation with the Trinity, giving thanks. Our Father.

Suggested Prayer Time: 30 minutes

Preparation: 5 minutes. Opening Prayer: 1 minute. Desire: 1 minute. Prayer: 20 minutes. Conversation: 3 minutes. Listening Book after prayer: 10 minutes.

How to Give This Exercise

The title of this exercise is "Inner Peace." It is day one, Monday of Week One of this retreat. This exercise, and the exercises of the week, match imaginative contemplation with special prayer texts to create places where the receiver might find serenity, peace, newness, encouragement, and harmony.

Your receiver is asked to express the gifts of serenity and quiet, as if already received. This is a way to shape his or her desire for the same. If other gifts or feelings come to your receiver, he or she should leave the text and go with what is being given by that person of the Trinity. Nothing is forced in this prayer.

The prayer method is imaginative contemplation, likely new to your receiver. In the Prayer point, the prayer texts have to be read slowly. Then good pauses are needed for your receiver to imagine and pray, between the creation of place and each conversation with the Trinity.

New Prayer Method 2: Father at work in the world

Preparation	Immediately on waking, I rouse myself to sorrow by standing in the shoes of one who has seriously offended their partner, friend, or superior who has in the past given them many favors. I get dressed with thoughts like these.
	At my prayer place, I stand to consider how the Father is gazing at me with mercy. I make a gesture of reverence and humility.
Opening Prayer	I ask for the grace to direct my whole self to the service of the Father.
Desire	I desire the tender mercy of the Father, even though feeling embarrassment and confusion at how little I merit this mercy.
Prayer	I read the prayer texts to consider how the Father works.
	Then I consider one person who has become snared in a lifestyle of sinful choices or trapped because of one deadly sin. I imagine such a person or, knowing someone like this, I stand back to look objectively at his or her life.
	I see how this person's choices created a darkness that moved through his or her life, at home and work, how he or she became unfree, cut off from life. I consider how the person's actions move against his or her lifelong fundamental goodness. I watch how destructive these choices and actions are to others, how they hurt children and families, even how corrosive of past good. I understand this person might be justly condemned. Perhaps I have even grieved to see it.
	Now I imagine the effects of the Father's infinite mercy in this person. I watch forgiveness flow through his or her fundamental goodness and see it reawaken. I catch love mending self-worth and watch generosity bud on half-dead relationships. Slowly, a life turns around. All undeserved, sustaining kindness is given in the face of its opposite. I go over this movement of mercy in more detail with my understanding, arousing my feelings as well.
Conversation	I conclude by imagining Christ before me on the cross. I ask him why he, Lord of all creation, became human, and why he loved me and why he was killed.
	Then, I ask myself, "What have I done for Christ? What

am I doing for Christ? What ought I to do for Christ?"

Still seeing him on the cross, I go over whatever comes to mind. Our Father.

Suggested Prayer Time: 35 minutes

Preparation: 3 minutes. Opening Prayer: 1 minute. Desire: 1 minute. Prayer: 20 minutes. Conversation: 10 minutes. Listening Book after Prayer: 10 minutes.

How to Give This Exercise

The title of this exercise is "Father at work in the world." It is day seven, Monday of Week Two of this retreat. The prayer method is imaginative contemplation. Ignatius goes into great detail in this week, carefully guiding both the method and the content. He assumes everyone is a learner. So the same long, detailed, systematic steps of imaginative contemplation are deliberately used in the exercises of this week.

As you read through the exercise, to guide your receiver, pause at appropriate places to give her or him time to imagine the scene and place themselves in it. Be sure your receiver leaves time for the conversation at the end of this exercise; they are especially important this week.

New Prayer Method 3: Light and darkness

Preparation	Immediately on waking, I rouse myself to urgency, seeing Jesus ready to show me the real effects of both love and sin. I get dressed with thoughts like these.
	At my prayer place, I stand to consider how Jesus is gazing at me with mercy. I make a gesture of reverence and humility.
Opening Prayer	I ask for the grace to direct my whole self to the service of Jesus.
Desire	I ask for an interior sense of the joy felt by those in heaven so that, if lost, powerless, or tempted, I will always remember the love of my eternal Lord.
Prayer	I read the prayer texts to see how actions of love and sin have very real effects.

The first step is to see with the eyes of the imagination, the length, breadth, and height, and depth of heaven—what is it like? What might I experience?

1. I look with the eyes of my imagination at the great heart of God, at the dance of the risen receiving and giving love. What else do I see?

2. I hear with my ears laughter, bird song, praises, waterfalls, music and conversations between Jesus and my family and friends. What else do I hear?

3. I smell with my sense of smell new cut grass, the sea, home-cooked food, spring breezes, fragrant oils and the newborn. What else do I smell?

4. I taste with my sense of taste the sweet things, like homecoming, a stolen kiss, a birthday, a child's wonder, harmony in conscience. What else do I taste?

5. I feel with my sense of touch the caress of intimacy in the Trinity. I feel whole and healed in my body. I embrace those I love. What else touches me?

The second step is to imagine, with the same five senses, the opposite of the above, what I might experience through the effects of sinfulness. So the image of hell, eternal aloneness, the endless bray of the selfish, the stink of evil, etc.

The third step is to consider how both these realities and effects are here on earth, the first in the growing kingdom of God where the hungry, thirsty, sick, naked, and imprisoned are cared for, and the second in the places where we see "hell on earth." In this vision,

God sets before me life and death, to be a life giver or a life destroyer, now and eternally. Which do I choose?

Conversation   I talk to Jesus, grateful that death has not taken my life. I thank him for his constant, loving kindness, right up to the present moment. Our Father.

Suggested Prayer Time: 35 minutes

Preparation: 5 minutes. Opening Prayer: 1 minute. Desire: 1 minute. Prayer: 20 minutes. Conversation: 8 minutes. Listening Book after prayer: 10 minutes.

How to Give This Exercise

The title of this exercise is "Light and darkness." It is day nine, Wednesday of Week Two of this retreat. The method of prayer is called the Prayer of the Interior Senses. See an explanation in The Ignatian Guide to Twelve Ways of Prayer in *The First Spiritual Exercises*. The key here is to guide each sense with a few descriptive words and let your receiver use her or his imagination, not yours. Leave enough time between each sense for your receiver to animate the scene, and for the Spirit to embellish it.

New Prayer Method 4: *EPHPHATHA*! Be opened!

Preparation	Immediately on waking, I rouse myself to hope by seeing myself as a deaf person, getting ready to go with friends to the roadside, knowing that Jesus will be passing by. I will get dressed with thoughts like these.

At my prayer place, I stand to consider how Jesus is gazing at me with gentle compassion. I make a gesture of reverence and humility.

Opening Prayer   I ask for the grace to direct my whole self to service of Jesus the healer.

Desire   I desire to see, hear, and speak clearly.

Prayer   I read each of the prayer texts to know how Jesus healed the blind and deaf.

Then I choose *one* of the three healing stories for my prayer. I enter the scene, imagining in some detail the place, weather, people, conversations, and sounds. I experience the actions and feelings as they unfold.

1. If I feel deaf and dumb in a relationship or work situation, I take the place of the deaf and dumb man brought to Jesus. I enter the gospel scene. I sense my friends begging Jesus to lay hands on me. I hear him say, "*Ephphatha!*" that is, "Be opened!" as he opens my ears and tongue. I allow the story to unfold. I hear my first sounds; I speak in wonder.

2. If I feel blind, in some way, wrapped in a cloak, and reduced to sitting on the side of life's road, I take the place of Bartimaeus. I enter the gospel scene. I yell to get the attention of Jesus, "Jesus, Son of David, have mercy on me!" I allow the story to unfold. Now I see.

3. If I have a chronic illness, draining relationship, or prolonged suffering, I take the place of the blind man guided to Jesus. I enter the gospel scene. I hear Jesus asking, "Can you see anything?" I relive the experience of being half- healed, in a halfway place, half alive. I allow the story to unfold. I see clearly.

Then, I surrender my vulnerabilities and healing to the Lord, that he may better work through me. I offer, if he wills, to help heal and encourage others.

Conversation	I give thanks to God for my faith, the gift that Jesus declares "makes me well."
	We share our feelings and thoughts. Our Father.

Suggested Prayer Time: 40 minutes

Preparation: 5 minutes. Opening Prayer: 1 minute. Desire: 1 minute. Prayer: 30 minutes. Conversation: 3 minutes. Listening Book after prayer: 10 minutes.

How to Give This Exercise

The title of this exercise is *"Ephphatha*! Be Opened!" It is day thirteen, Monday of Week Three of this retreat. The prayer method is imaginative contemplation. All the prayer texts are read but your receiver chooses only *one* healing relationship to pray.

Jesus, words of healing, as found in the gospels, are often exclamations. In your guiding you might give the exercise with similar power, energy, and wonder.

Please note, if this prayer takes your receiver to a past event that still holds a lot of suffering, advise your receiver to not become submerged in the event, else he or she can be trapped and replay all its feelings. Rather, have your receiver stand outside the scene with Jesus, deliberately detached, and gently talking to him about then and now.

New Prayer Method 5: Praise

1. I enter into the Gift of Praise.

    I read the prayer texts to contemplate the reality of praise.

    I imagine myself in the relationships, becoming the lame man, Elizabeth, Mary or Jesus.

    I awaken my praised and praising heart.

2. I ask the Holy Spirit for help.

    I ask for guidance in this spiritual exercise.

3. I review and journal my experience of praise.

    How, when and for what do others praise me?

    How, when and for what do I praise myself?

    How, when and for what does the Lord praise me?

4. I respond to what has emerged.

    I express to Jesus how I feel when I am praised or praising.

    I seek to understand how praise will enhance life.

    I praise him.

5. I choose for the future.

    I contemplate my journal to see what patterns have emerged in answering point three above:

    > Are there similar gifts? Revealing differences?

    > What consoles me or enlivens me? What desolates or deadens me?

    > Which gifts, revealed in praise, are the most important to me? Those I can do without?

    I note these patterns, insights, and priorities in my Listening Book. Our Father.

Suggested Prayer Time: 40 minutes

Enter the gift of praise: 10 minutes. Ask the Holy Spirit for help: 2 minutes. Listening Book: 13 minutes. Respond: 5 minutes. Choose: 10 minutes.

How to Give This Exercise

The title of this exercise is "Praise." It is day nineteen, Monday of Week Four of this retreat. This exercise is repeated three times, beginning with praise and then replacing praise with reverence and then with service. Explain to your receiver the need to use his or her Listening Book for responses to the questions asked in the third point. Essentially you are guiding him or her to recall life experiences of praise, reverence and service. In point five, your receiver uses the notes made in point three to find patterns and make priorities.

In the fourth exercise, you give your receiver four versions of the Foundation text, of which one is chosen. Each text is broken up into four clear parts. If this retreat is given to a group, the four Foundation texts may be read to great effect by reading part one in each text, and then part two in each text, etc. Each version enlightens the others and so the meaning of the whole Foundation.

After a Foundation text is chosen, your receiver uses her or his Listening Book to listen to the insights of the previous three exercises noted under point five. She or he does this under point three of the exercise. Then in point five, your receiver chooses two practical actions.

It would be difficult to guide this exercise by voice. Rather, go through the steps required in the exercises this week, answer any questions, and let your receiver make the exercises alone. Stress to your receiver that time is needed to ponder each question in turn, in both the third and fifth points of the exercises. The answers will be revealing.

4. Images of God in Action

Ignatius was well aware of how open one's consciousness is upon waking. So he asks your receiver to hold, for just a moment, the desire or divine relationship wished for that day. Then, he or she is to "get dressed with thoughts like these."

Getting dressed.	In the preparation steps
Week One	I rouse my desire for inner peace by imagining Jesus calming the sea around me.
	I rouse myself to joy by imagining the new life I need is coming today.
	I rouse myself to hope by imagining Jesus encouraging me everywhere today.
Week Two	I rouse myself to sorrow by standing in the shoes of one who has seriously offended their partner, friend or superior who has in the past given them many favors.
	I rouse myself to sorrow by seeing myself chained, immobilized and dying by my own choices, before the very Spirit who gave me life and freedom.
	I rouse myself to urgency, seeing Jesus ready to show me the real effects of both love and sin.
	I rouse myself to hope by recalling that, from birth, Jesus has never stopped loving me.
Week Three	I rouse myself to hope by seeing myself as a deaf person, getting ready to go with friends to the roadside, knowing Jesus will be passing by.
	I rouse myself to hope by imagining Jesus asking me, "Do you want to be made well?"
	I rouse myself to hope by imagining I am possessed and tormented, yet realize that Jesus desires to free me today.
	I rouse myself to hope by seeing myself as one dead, hearing the Lord calling me by name, saying, "Take heart! I will raise you to life."
Week Four	I rouse myself to joy by imagining Jesus delighted with my Program for Life.

In the early life of the Christian community, there were short prayers carried on one breath a phrase to hold desire and the whole self before God. Prayers of desire are also found on the lips of God.

Prayers of desire	In the prayer texts
Week One	I have called you by name, you are mine.
	You are precious in my sight, and honored, and I love you.
	Do not let your heart be afraid.
	O Lord, my eyes are not raised too high.
	Receive the Holy Spirit.
Week Two	Have mercy on me, O God, according to your steadfast love.
	Teach me wisdom in my secret heart.
	O God, put a new and right spirit within me.
	Father, into your hands I commend my spirit.
	God, be merciful to me, a sinner!
	Father, I am no longer worthy to be called your son.
Week Three	*Ephphatha*! Be opened!
	Jesus, Son of David, have mercy on me!
	My teacher, let me see again.
	Come out of the man, you unclean spirit!
	Teacher, but if you are able to do anything, have pity on us and help us.
	I believe; help my unbelief!
	Talitha cum! Little girl, get up!
	Young man, I say to you, rise!
	Roll back the stone. Unbind him, and let him go.
Week Four	My soul magnifies the Lord, and my spirit rejoices in God my Savior.
	This is my Son, with whom I am well pleased.

Giving Inner Peace in Friendship with Jesus

This is my commandment,
that you love one another
as I have loved you.
No one has greater love than this,
to lay down one's life for one's friends.
You are my friends
if you do what I command you. . . .
I have called you friends,
because I have made known to you
everything that I have heard from my Father.
You did not choose me but I chose you.
And I appointed you to go and bear fruit,
fruit that will last,
so that the Father will give you
whatever you ask him in my name.
—John 15:12–16

1. The Purpose of This Retreat

The purpose of this retreat is to bring your receiver into a working relationship with Jesus and so deepen his or her friendship with him. During it, your receiver will experience how Jesus befriends others in the truest ways, through acceptance, sharing, listening, forgiving, loving and so on. Then the receiver brings to mind someone he or she knows in need of friendship, and is a friend to that person in the same way as Jesus is to him or her. So the purpose of this retreat is to experience a friendship with Jesus born of two people having the same desires and working together.

Friendship between the Trinity and your receiver is a profound part of creation, incarnation, love, resurrection and eternal life. It underpins the big story of the universe. So the purpose of the first and last week is to help your receiver to enter the big story of creation and discover her or his connections to it. The middle weeks are more intimate; your receiver enters into the close friendship of Jesus as a coworker, the purpose being to deepen that friendship.

The use of a symbol in each exercise gives your receiver a way to hold and touch the heart of each prayer. The symbol suffuses the life of your receiver with the desired aspect of friendship. Sometime in this retreat, Jesus will breathe the Spirit into your receiver to banish fear and break through obstacles, so that he or she may have a vital, peaceful, working friendship with him.

Retreat Map

Note in this map how all four examens are given and how the exercises that proceed them use them.

WEEK ONE	JESUS, A FRIEND FOR CREATION
Monday	The Spirit hovers over creation.
Tuesday	The Father raises life in the universe.
Wednesday	The Son is born *Homo sapiens*.
Thursday	I am born in the image of God.
Saturday	Awareness Examen
Sunday	I desire divine relationship.

WEEK TWO	JESUS, A FRIEND FOR EVERY DAY
Monday	Jesus shows me how friends accept.
Tuesday	Jesus shows me how friends receive.
Wednesday	Jesus shows me how friends share.
Thursday	Jesus shows me how friends heal.
Saturday	Healing Examen
Sunday	I desire divine life.

WEEK THREE	JESUS, A FRIEND FOR EVERY TIME
Monday	Jesus shows me how friends listen.
Tuesday	Jesus shows me how friends forgive.
Wednesday	Jesus shows me how friends work.
Thursday	Jesus shows me how friends love.
Saturday	Reconciliation Examen
Sunday	I desire divine intimacy.

WEEK FOUR	JESUS, A FRIEND FOR LIFE
Monday	The Father raises my friend to life.
Tuesday	The Spirit hovers over the friends of Jesus.
Wednesday	The Son calls his friends home.
Thursday	Program for Life
Saturday	Particular Examen
Sunday	I desire divine friendship.

Desires Map

In this map, "with Jesus" means to work with Jesus.

WEEK ONE	JESUS, A FRIEND FOR CREATION
Monday	I desire to know the creative God.
Tuesday	I desire to know the life-giving God.
Wednesday	I desire to know the human God.
Thursday	I desire to know the personal God.
Sunday	I desire divine relationship.

WEEK TWO	JESUS, A FRIEND FOR EVERY DAY
Monday	I desire to accept with Jesus.
Tuesday	I desire to receive with Jesus.
Wednesday	I desire to share with Jesus.
Thursday	I desire to heal with Jesus.
Sunday	I desire divine life.

WEEK THREE	JESUS, A FRIEND FOR EVERY TIME
Monday	I desire to listen with Jesus.
Tuesday	I desire to forgive with Jesus.
Wednesday	I desire to work with Jesus.
Thursday	I desire to love with Jesus.
Sunday	I desire divine intimacy.

WEEK FOUR	JESUS, A FRIEND FOR LIFE
Monday	I desire living hope from the Father.
Tuesday	I desire fire from the Spirit.
Wednesday	I desire resurrection with Jesus.
Thursday	I desire a Program for Life.
Sunday	I desire divine friendship.

2. Content and Dynamic

WEEK ONE	JESUS, A FRIEND FOR CREATION	
Monday	The Spirit hovers over creation.	
Tuesday	The Father raises life in the universe.	
Wednesday	The Son is born *Homo sapiens*.	
Thursday	I am born in the image of God.	
Saturday	Awareness Examen	
Sunday	I desire divine relationship.	Eucharist

The content this week is the big picture of a friendship with Jesus. It is found in this and the last week of the retreat. So the retreat moves from the beginning of everything, to your receiver's life with Jesus, to the eternal life of everything. It is a universal contemplation of friendship with Jesus.

Step 1. The Vision

> The great visions this week are of creation, life, evolution, the Incarnation, and your receiver's birth, each one flowing into the other. This is the content. The dynamic is the opening of eyes wide open, increasing breadth of imagination, and growing wonder at the friendship of God.

Step 2. The Relationships

> In this step your receiver considers the relationships that follow from the preceding vision. The dynamic is creating connections. The content is the reality of the relationships and your receiver's answer to the question, "What difference does this relationship make to you?"

Step 3. Colloquy of the Senses

> The content of this step is a "colloquy" or "conversation" between God and your receiver. Your receiver is asked to take a symbol, to bless and hold, as she or he converses with God. Because a symbol engages all the senses, this step is called a "colloquy of the senses." The dynamic here is a profound exploration of friendship with the Trinity and Jesus. Although the symbols change with each exercise, they have a cumulative dynamic, each adding richness to the others. For example, earth and water seem right to hold in each hand, both symbolizing so much of

creation. To conclude the dynamic of the week, Sunday brings together the week's symbols.

WEEK TWO	JESUS, A FRIEND FOR EVERY DAY	
Monday	Jesus shows me how friends accept.	Awareness Examen
Tuesday	Jesus shows me how friends receive.	Awareness Examen
Wednesday	Jesus shows me how friends share.	Awareness Examen
Thursday	Jesus shows me how friends heal.	Awareness Examen
Saturday	Healing Examen	
Sunday	I desire divine life.	Eucharist

The content this week takes your receiver into core experiences of friendship, those of accepting, receiving, sharing and healing. The first two steps reflect that friendship is built on common desires. It grows when friends do things together and new friendships are created when what is received is given and shared with another. This is the essential dynamic of this week and next.

Step 1. Jesus accepts me.

Your receiver takes the place of the one in relationship with Jesus. The event provides the content. The dynamic is that your receiver has knowledge from this exercise to take into the next step.

Step 2. As a friend of Jesus, I accept others.

Your receiver responds to others as Jesus has responded to her or him. Using imagination and memory, your receiver recalls a person he or she knows. The dynamic unfolds, with one giving what one has received, and your receiver experiences in real life how working with Jesus feels.

Step 3. I see my part in the great unfolding story of divine friendship.

This step invites your receiver to imagine, in detail, how one action in life has great consequences. She or he sees this small act set off a chain of relationships and events that reaches deep into the future. This is friendship with Jesus in action.

Step 4. Colloquy of the Senses.

This last step is identical to the previous week in dynamic and content.

WEEK THREE	JESUS, A FRIEND FOR EVERY TIME	
Monday	Jesus shows me how friends listen.	Awareness Examen
Tuesday	Jesus shows me how friends forgive.	Awareness Examen
Wednesday	Jesus shows me how friends work.	Awareness Examen
Thursday	Jesus shows me how friends love.	Awareness Examen
Saturday	Reconciliation Examen	
Sunday	I desire divine intimacy.	Eucharist

This week the exercises move through powerful movements of listening, forgiving, working and loving in friendship. The dynamic of experiencing what may be enjoyed in a friendship with Jesus grows, as does appreciation of the depths a friendship with Jesus can reach for your receiver.

This week and the last, and often entwined, you will hear the deeper life stories and desires of your receiver. Often the opposite of what is desired surfaces in memory—a friendship lost, a healing not found, a dying still in progress. Here your own friendship with your receiver, grown in the course of this retreat, can gently support him or her through reverent listening and conversation. Here too is precisely where Jesus most wishes to be a friend for your receiver.

The additional dynamic this week for your receiver moves toward a more realistic friendship with Jesus and an understanding of the things that might tug him or her away from it.

WEEK FOUR	JESUS, A FRIEND FOR LIFE	
Monday	The Father raises my friend to life.	Awareness Examen
Tuesday	The Spirit hovers over the friends of Jesus.	
Wednesday	The Son calls his friends home.	Awareness Examen
Thursday	Program for Life	
Saturday	Particular Examen	
Sunday	I desire divine friendship.	Eucharist

This week your receiver explores the promises of divine friendship: life from death, being sent out to serve, and promised a home for eternity. Your receiver has now been through the full circle of creation, incarnation, friendship, death, resurrection and eternal life. This is the grand dynamic of the retreat. There are also intimate moments, for this loving friendship grows from the roots of the universe, through every lived day, and remains up to the last murmured thanks.

The particular dynamic of the week is found in the three steps below.

Step 1. A Promise Fulfilled

The first part of the exercise is imaginative contemplation. But rather than guiding your receiver through a whole event, you give her or him a starting place to pray from, a flash of the scene from whence they move. In this step, the content is really provided by your receiver.

Step 2. New Friends

Your receiver imagines a place of serenity. Jesus introduces your receiver to the Father, Spirit, and Communion of Saints and asks each to be your receiver's friend. This is the content. After this intimate moment, the dynamic flows into friends enjoying each other's company in quiet peace.

Step 3. Colloquy of the Senses

The colloquy remains the same as before, but the last exercise of the retreat uses all fifteen symbols in one great circle. The dynamic is to feel the progressive graces of the whole retreat, for your receiver to sit in the circle of divine friendship, remembering and receiving. It makes for a joyful conclusion.

3. New Prayer Methods

New Prayer Method 1: The Spirit hovers over creation.

Preparation | At my prayer place, I consider how the Spirit hovers over me in her work of continuing creation. I make a gesture of reverence and humility.

I read the prayer texts to anchor myself in the power of divine creativity.

Opening Prayer | With simple words, I offer my whole self to the Spirit.

Desire | I desire to know the creative God.

Prayer | With my imagination, I contemplate the creation of the universe.

First, the vision—I imagine the creation of the Universe, 13.7 billion years ago. I see the big bang and the creation of particles and antiparticles, the fundamental forces of gravity, electromagnetism, strong and weak nuclear forces, and the prodigious expansion of everything.

I see, in my own way, protons and neutrons binding in the cooling universe to form hydrogen and helium nuclei, until, at 300,000 years, the first atoms form and photons of light are released in a sea of radiation. I see the Spirit above and in everything, even direction itself. I hear, "Let there be light!"

Then, over eons, I see all the elements being progressively created in stars, evermore complex in the burning hearts and explosive deaths.

Second, the relationship—I consider my profound relationship to the beginning of creation. I drink a glass of water. In it I am drinking the hydrogen created in the first moment of creation—for all hydrogen around and within me was created then and none since. I can say, in a very real way, that part of me was there in the beginning.

Every other element in my body was created in generations of stars. Physically, I carry the story of creation within me.

What difference does this make to the way I relate to universe?

Colloquy of the Senses	In reverence, I take a bowl of water, symbol of the waters of creation. I bless it.
	I gently blow over the face of the water, asking myself how I might join in the Spirit's work of loving creation.
	I conclude, in conversation, as with a friend, by sharing my thoughts and feelings with the Holy Spirit.
	Our Father.

Suggested Prayer Time: 40 minutes

Preparation, Opening Prayer, Desire: 10 minutes. Prayer: 20 minutes. Colloquy of the Senses: 10 minutes. Listening Book after prayer: 10 minutes.

How to Give This Exercise

The title of this exercise is "The Spirit hovers over creation." It is day one, Monday of Week One of this retreat.

Step 1. The Vision

The first step is a prayer of imaginative contemplation. Before beginning, tell your receiver that scientific knowledge is unnecessary. The big bang, etc., can be imagined as she or he wills. Guide your receiver slowly to realize the scene; then give five minutes to ponder the vision.

Step 2. The Relationship

The second step is a prayer of consideration. You guide your receiver through the consideration of the relationship, leaving time for actions where necessary. Leave time for the question at the end.

Step 3. Colloquy of the Senses

The third step is a prayer of the senses. Have your receiver keep her or his eyes closed for this exercise until the colloquy of the senses. Then invite your receiver to open her or his eyes and take up the symbol. Time and reverence are needed here for your receiver to hold, bless and experience the symbol. Give time for the last question and the final conversation.

In the Sunday exercise all four symbols are gathered to review the graces of the week. A practical note: you need to give your receiver a list of the fifteen symbols before the retreat. It is very important that he or she brings them from home, for after the retreat the symbols will continue to be potent where they are most needed, in your receiver's home. This week the symbols are:

1. Bowl of water   Water of creation

2. Bowl of garden earth   Earth of life

3. Grandparent's family object   Deep family time

4. Hand mirror   Mirror of God

New Prayer Method 2: Jesus shows me how friends accept.

Preparation	Immediately on waking, I recall people I know who need acceptance and imagine bringing them to Jesus. I get dressed with thoughts like these.
	At my prayer place, I make a gesture of reverence and humility.
Opening Prayer	I ask for the grace to direct my whole self to the Jesus who accepts the burdened.
Desire	I desire to accept with Jesus.
Prayer	I read the prayer texts to see how Jesus accepts. Then, in three steps I pray.

1. Jesus accepts me. I choose *one* of the accepting relationships in the prayer texts. I use my imagination to enter the scene as the one in need. I fill in the details of people and conversation. I come to Jesus and let the scene unfold.

2. As a friend of Jesus, I accept others. I use my imagination to bring before me a person I know who yearns to be accepted. I imagine a place and what we might say. I let the scene unfold as I befriend and accept like Jesus.

3. I see my part in the great unfolding story of divine friendship, creation, salvation and eternal life. Standing back, I imagine, in detail, the effects of my acceptance of the other radiating forward into the long future. I see more and more people, communities, and even earth and its creatures becoming utterly welcomed, accepted and called into the living realm of God.

Colloquy of the Senses	In reverence, I take a jar of ointment as a symbol of acceptance. I bless it.
	Removing my shoes, I anoint and massage my feet with ointment. Then Jesus and I share how we feel about our friendship. We consider how to bring acceptance to those I have remembered in this prayer.
	Our Father.

Suggested Prayer Time: 40 minutes

Preparation and Desire: 5 minutes. Prayer Step 1: 10 minutes. Prayer Step 2: 10 minutes. Prayer Step 3: 5 minutes. Colloquy of the Senses: 10 minutes. Listening Book after prayer: 10 minutes.

How to Give This Exercise

The title of this exercise is "Jesus shows me how friends accept." It is day seven, Monday of Week Two of this retreat. Each exercise begins with a morning rise awareness prayer. The three parts of the Prayer need about ten minutes each. The prayer method is the same for this week and the next.

Step 1. Jesus accepts me.

> The first step is an imaginative contemplation. Instruct your receiver to chose only *one* of the prayer texts to enter. Guide her or him slowly into the scene and leave them in silence.

Step 2. As a friend of Jesus, I accept others.

> Again using imaginative contemplation, guide your receiver through this step.

Step 3. I see my part in the great unfolding story of divine friendship, creation, salvation, and eternal life.

> In this step your receiver imagines the effects of their action in step two unfold and ripple into the future. Your receiver will need a little time to see it all happen and ponder.

Step 4. Colloquy of the Senses.

> This step is basically the same as the previous week. What is new is the conversation between your receiver and Jesus about their friendship, and how they might both help the person in need.

The symbols for Week Two:

5. Ointment	Ointment of acceptance
6. Foot towel	Foot towel of receiving
7. Loaf of bread	Bread of sharing
8. Oil	Oil of healing

9. Seeds   Seeds of listening

10. Ring   Ring of joyous forgiveness

11. Fruit   Fruit of work

12. Cross   Cross of love

New Prayer Method 3: The Father raises my friend to life.

Preparation	At my prayer place, I consider how the Father raises the dead to life. I make a gesture of reverence and humility.
	I read the prayer texts to understand the outcome of divine friendship.
Opening Prayer	With simple words, I offer my whole self to the Father.
Desire	I desire living hope from the Father.
Prayer	With my imagination, I see the consequences of friendship with Jesus:
	First, a promise fulfilled—I use my imagination to stand in the small tomb of Jesus. It is pitch dark, yet as dawn breaks, beams of dusty, golden light slip past the round stone at my back. Gradually I make out the dead body of Jesus; his wounds are clear, his binding cloths folded at his feet. Suddenly, his whole back arches, ribs stretched, head thrown back, arms pressed to the stone. He takes the first great, shuddering breath of new life. His eyes snap open. He exhales slowly, settling down, deeply weighted in the here and now—alive.
	He becomes aware of me, turns his head and speaks my name.
	I allow the rest of his resurrection to unfold around me.
	Second, new friends—Next, I use my imagination to create a place of serenity to abide in—a place of peaceful habitation, a secure dwelling, a quiet resting place (Is 32:18). It may be in a forest, garden, mountain, beach or home. Here I sit with the risen Jesus and his Father. Jesus personally asks the Father to be my friend. The Father welcomes me with indescribable joy, and fills my heart with laughter. Then, as it is with closest friends, we sit in companionable quiet together, enjoying each other's presence.
Colloquy of the Senses	In reverence, I take an article of new clothing, symbol of resurrection. I bless it and put it on.
	Then, clothed in Christ, Jesus and I share how we feel about our friendship.
	I ask myself how I might join in his work of bringing new life from death.
	Our Father.

Suggested Prayer Time: 40 minutes

Preparation, Opening Prayer, Desire: 10 minutes. Prayer: 20 minutes. Conversation: 10 minutes. Listening Book after prayer: 10 minutes.

How to Give This Exercise

The title of this exercise is "The Father raises my friend to life." It is day nineteen, Monday of Week Four of this retreat. This exercise introduces the last new prayer method for the retreat.

Step 1. A Promise Fulfilled

> The exercise sets the scene. Your receiver is then invited to complete it. Guide your receiver to this point, then give him or her about ten minutes to allow the event to unfold in his or her imagination.

Step 2. New Friends

> Your receiver imagines a place of serenity where she or he is introduced to the Trinity. Give your receiver time to set the scene each day, receive new friends and sit in companionable silence.

Step 3. Colloquy of the Senses

> Consider the combination of symbols. This happens naturally, but if helpful to your receiver, you might suggest it. What if, for example, your receiver washed her or his feet with the water of creation, dried them with the towel of receiving and anointed each foot with the ointment of acceptance?

> In the Sunday exercise all fifteen symbols are brought together. Invite your receiver to make a large circle of them and sit in it to review and feel the full graciousness of friendship with Jesus.

> This week the symbols are:

> 13. New clothing   Clothing of resurrection

> 14. Hand-size candle Fire of the Spirit

> 15. House keys   Home keys of heaven

4. Images of God in Action

Each pause before a prayer place, each waking thought, can be a miniature prayer. In weeks one and four, your receiver stands before one of the Trinity. In weeks two and three, your receiver considers one in need, known personally, and brings that person to Jesus.

In the preparation steps

WEEK ONE   I consider how the Spirit hovers over me in her work of continuing creation.

I consider how the Father grew me out of stars, the earth, evolution and womb.

I consider how Jesus, as *Homo sapiens*, a human being, shares in my humanity.

I consider how my Creator sees me as very good.

WEEK TWO   I recall people I know who need acceptance and imagine bringing them to Jesus.

I recall people I know who have much to give me and imagine bringing them to Jesus.

I recall people I know who are in need and imagine bringing them to Jesus.

I recall people I know who need healing and imagine bringing them to Jesus.

WEEK THREE   I recall people I know who need a good listener and imagine bringing them to Jesus.

I recall people I know who need forgiveness and imagine bringing them to Jesus.

I recall people I know who need God's action in their life, and imagine bringing them to Jesus.

I recall people I know who need love and imagine bringing them to Jesus.

WEEK FOUR   I consider how the Father raises the dead to life.

I consider how the Spirit hovers over me, kindling in me the fire of God's love.

I consider how I am created to live for eternity.

I consider how Jesus is looking at me as a friend.

Fifteen symbols of divine friendship

The last moment in the colloquy of the senses sees two friends, two co-workers. I talking about how they might work together. This includes the questions below.

WEEK ONE	Water of creation	How might I join in the Spirit's work of creation?
	Earth of life	How might I join in God's work of nurturing life?
	Family object	How might I join God's work of evolving humanity?
	Mirror of God	How might I better reflect who I am?
WEEK TWO	Ointment of acceptance	How might I accept those remembered in prayer?
	Foot towel of receiving	How to receive from those remembered in prayer?
	Bread of sharing	How might I share with those remembered in prayer?
	Oil of healing	How might I heal those remembered in prayer?
WEEK THREE	Seeds of listening	How might I listen to those remembered in prayer?
	Ring of joyous forgiveness	How might I forgive those remembered in prayer?
	Fruit of work	How might I work for those remembered in prayer?
	Cross of love	How might I love those remembered in prayer?
WEEK FOUR	Clothing of resurrection	How might I join in Jesus' work of giving life?
	Fire of the Spirit	How might I serve with the gifts of the Spirit?
	House keys of heaven	How might I live, knowing my final destination?

GIVING INNER PEACE IN SERVICE OF GOD

Be filled

with the knowledge of God's will

in all spiritual wisdom

and understanding,

so that you may lead lives

worthy of the Lord,

fully pleasing to him,

as you bear fruit

in every good work

and as you grow

in the knowledge of God.

—Colossians 1:9–11

1. The Purpose of This Retreat

In 1527, Ignatius gave the exercises of this retreat to help people better serve God. Two women, Leonor and Beatriz, were among them and we hear their voices through the transcripts of the Inquisition interviews made of the spiritual conversations and exercises being given by Ignatius in Alcalá.

> And [the Inquisitor] asked [Leonor] whether she had listened to Yñigo and what he had taught her. She replied that Yñigo had taught her the commandments of the Church and the five senses and other things for the service of God. (Leonor de Mena, March 6, 1527)

> Yñigo was giving doctrine on the first two commandments, how it was necessary to know and love God, etc., and about this he spoke at length; and that this witness found herself amongst these people, and was overwhelmed in seeing that what Yñigo talked about were things, not new to this witness, but about loving God and one's neighbor, etc. (Beatriz Ramirez, November 21, 1527)

Here is the birth of this retreat. The purpose of the first week is to help your receiver discover meaning and find relish in her or his faith. It prepares the ground. The second week takes your receiver deeper into divine relationships. The third and fourth weeks elicit particular and deeply personal ways to serve God and neighbor.

The four Sunday exercises ask your receiver to consider the service of others through the Body of Christ. Finally, a Program for Life charts how your receiver may serve God.

Retreat Map

WEEK ONE	PROGRESS THROUGH DELIGHT
Monday	Awareness Examen
Tuesday	Delight and meaning in the Father
Wednesday	Delight and meaning in Mary
Thursday	Delight and meaning in my faith
Sunday	Food in the Body of Christ

WEEK TWO	PROGRESS THROUGH RELATIONSHIP
Monday	Breathing in the Father
Tuesday	Breathing in the Soul of Christ
Wednesday	Breathing in the Spirit
Thursday	Breathing in the Creator
Sunday	Life in the Body of Christ

WEEK THREE	PROGRESS THROUGH DESIRE
Monday	Particular Examen
Tuesday	Progress through the new commandments
Wednesday	Progress through the Beatitudes
Thursday	Progress through the virtues
Saturday	Reconciliation Examen
Sunday	Ligament in the Body of Christ

WEEK FOUR	PROGRESS THROUGH SERVICE
Monday	Progress through the gifts of the Spirit
Tuesday	Progress through the gifts of the body
Wednesday	Progress through the works of mercy
Thursday	Program for Life
Sunday	Service in the Body of Christ

Desires Map

WEEK ONE	PROGRESS THROUGH DELIGHT
Monday	Awareness Examen
Tuesday	To find delight and meaning in the Father
Wednesday	To find delight and meaning in Mary
Thursday	To find delight and meaning in my faith
Sunday	I desire living bread in the Body of Christ.

WEEK TWO	PROGRESS THROUGH RELATIONSHIP
Monday	I desire to breathe in the Father.
Tuesday	I desire to breathe in the Soul of Christ.
Wednesday	I desire to breathe in the Spirit.
Thursday	I desire to breathe in the Creator.
Sunday	I desire life in the Body of Christ.

WEEK THREE	PROGRESS THROUGH DESIRE
Monday	Particular Examen
Tuesday	I desire spiritual progress in the new commandments.
Wednesday	I desire spiritual progress in the Beatitudes.
Thursday	I desire spiritual progress in the virtues.
Saturday	Reconciliation Examen
Sunday	I desire to be a ligament in the Body of Christ.

WEEK FOUR	PROGRESS THROUGH SERVICE
Monday	I desire spiritual progress in the gifts of the Spirit.
Tuesday	I desire spiritual progress in the gifts of the body.
Wednesday	I desire spiritual progress in the works of mercy.
Thursday	I desire to create a Program for Life.
Sunday	I desire to serve in the Body of Christ.

2. Content and Dynamic

WEEK ONE	PROGRESS THROUGH DELIGHT	
Monday	Awareness Examen	
Tuesday	Delight and meaning in the Father	Awareness Examen
Wednesday	Delight and meaning in Mary	Awareness Examen
Thursday	Delight and meaning in my faith	Awareness Examen
Sunday	Food in the Body of Christ	Eucharist

This week your receiver prays each word in five ancient prayers; the Our Father, Hail Mary, Apostles' Creed, Soul of Christ, and Come, Holy Spirit. Ignatius calls this the second way of praying (*Spiritual Exercises* 249–57). Deceptively simple, these exercises invite your receiver to find meanings, comparisons, relish and consolation in each word. He or she prays each word and the whole prayer, and then all five prayers in the normal way. This is the content of the week.

The dynamic is surprising—invisible in the text, it is only revealed in the doing. Your receiver will find in slowing down to pray a single word that the four aspects—meanings, comparisons, relish and consolation—become separate contemplations in themselves. In this dynamic, your receiver's mind catches meanings and comparisons, while her or his heart seeks relish and consolations.

The dynamic of a single prayer is that each word grows from the previous with increasing fruitfulness. In the dynamic of the four exercises this week, the graces and meaning of one word, in one ancient prayer, spill into similar words in the other ancient prayers. In a cyclic manner, with increasing connections, the stories, truths, memories and delights all enrich each other.

WEEK TWO	PROGRESS THROUGH RELATIONSHIP	
Monday	Breathing in the Father	Awareness Examen
Tuesday	Breathing in the Soul of Christ	Awareness Examen
Wednesday	Breathing in the Spirit	Awareness Examen
Thursday	Breathing in the Creator	Awareness Examen
Sunday	Life in the Body of Christ	Eucharist

This week continues from the first three ancient prayers to include the Soul of Christ and the Come, Holy Spirit, but using a different prayer method. More contemplatively, your receiver uses her or his breath to pray. Ignatius calls this the third way of praying (*Spiritual Exercises* 258–60).

The word *rûah* in Aramaic means Spirit, breath, wind, breeze, life and life of God. The one who hovers over creation is *rûah*. The breath that Jesus breathes into his disciples is *rûah*. The Spirit that the Lord sends forth to renew the earth is *rûah*. And life itself is *rûah*, "I have life within me, the breath of God in my nostrils" (Jb 27:3). This meaning of breath as life-giving, life renewing, and life divine is the dynamic that flows like breath itself through your receiver.

A background dynamic of the first two weeks is that your receiver is immersing him- or herself in the Father's kingdom, the mystery of the incarnation, core Christian beliefs, the death and resurrection of Jesus, and the gifts of the Spirit. So your receiver is always learning "where I am going and to what purpose" (*Spiritual Exercises* 239).

Thursday and Sunday exercises are new, to heighten union with the Creator and Body of Christ.

WEEK THREE	PROGRESS THROUGH DESIRE	
Monday	Particular Examen	
Tuesday	Progress in the new commandments	Particular Examen
Wednesday	Progress through the Beatitudes	Particular Examen
Thursday	Progress through the virtues	Particular Examen
Saturday	Reconciliation Examen	
Sunday	Ligament in the Body of Christ	Eucharist

This week your receiver prays the new commandments, Beatitudes, and virtues. Ignatius calls this the first way of praying (*Spiritual Exercises* 238–48). The exercises hold summaries of virtue and service. These graceful lists, found in the scriptures, are the content of the next two weeks.

Your receiver considers four questions for each gift on a list: What is it? Where is it present in her or his life? Where is it absent? What is its contrary? The dynamic is very personal, relevant, and arousing. This mini-cycle repeats with every gift on the list and then each day with different lists.

Ignatius says that for a better knowledge of each gift, your receiver could look at each gift's contraries; and similarly (and more surely to progress in a gift), he or she should resolve and endeavor by means of devout exercises to acquire the good of it and avoid the contrary evil (*Spiritual Exercises* 245).

The "contrary" may need explanation. Love and hate are contraries of one another. Desire and aversion are contraries, as are exultation and depression. These contraries are not just different or diverse; they are diametrically opposed. When I know one contrary I always know about the other. If I have experience of hate, I understand love better. This is the power of contraries; they give a startling clarity. And all contraries move in opposite directions. Ignatius invites your receiver to understand this him- or herself, and in the world, and to move in the direction of the good.

There are three final questions. The dynamic here is affirmation for your receiver and freedom to choose what would give both personal life and be of help to others.

WEEK FOUR	PROGRESS THROUGH SERVICE	
Monday	Progress through the gifts of the Spirit	Particular Examen
Tuesday	Progress through the gifts of the body	Particular Examen
Wednesday	Progress through the works of mercy	Particular Examen
Thursday	Program for Life	
Sunday	Service in the Body of Christ	Eucharist

The content of this week is the gifts of the Spirit, the gifts of the body, and the works of mercy. The dynamic is the same as last week; considerations for greater praise and service of God. At the end a Program for Life is created.

The Awareness Examen and the Particular Examen play an important role in this retreat. In the first two weeks, your receiver seeks God's love and power at work in all things, as revealed in the great sweep of the five ancient prayers. The evening Awareness Examen resonates with the day's focus. In the last two weeks, your receiver seeks God's love and power at work in one particular, chosen thing. She or he chooses to live courageously, to listen like Jesus, to feed the hungry, and so on.

3. New Prayer Methods

New Prayer Method 1: Delight and meaning in the Father

Preparation	I will allow my spirit to rest a little, and consider where I am going and for what purpose. I make a gesture of reverence and humility. I read the prayer texts.
Opening Prayer	I ask the Father for the grace to direct my whole self toward him.
Desire	I desire to find delight and meaning in the Father.
Prayer	Keeping my eyes closed, or fixed on one spot without wandering, I say the word "Our," staying with this word for as long as I find meanings, comparisons, relish, and consolation in considerations related to it. I do this for each word or sense phrase of the Our Father.
	I spend my whole prayer time on the Our Father. When I am finished I say the Our Father, Hail Mary, Apostles' Creed, Soul of Christ, and Come, Holy Spirit, aloud or silently, in the usual way.
Conversation	I ask the Father for the virtues or graces for which I feel the greatest need.

Suggested Prayer Time: 30 minutes

Preparation: 5 minutes. Opening Prayer: 1 minute. Desire: 1 minute. Prayer: 20 minutes. Conversation: 3 minutes. Listening Book after prayer: 10 minutes.

How to Give This Exercise

The title of this exercise is "Delight and meaning in the Father." It is day two, Tuesday of Week One of this retreat. The prayer texts, read in the preparation step, ground the content of each exercise in the gospels. The prayer method is the Prayer of Consideration. So the key to this exercise is the four considerations of each word: meanings, comparisons, relish and consolation.

The meaning of each word is straightforward. Comparisons means comparisons that illuminate the word. So for Father, your receiver might compare God the Father to his or her own father, or fathers and mothers, or being a parent like the Father, or how different fathers love and protect, or the lack of a father compared to one present, and so on. Relish is finding wonderful feelings, taste, tang, or delight in the reality of a word. Consolations mean spiritual consolations—so, joy, freedom, wonder, quiet peace, new hope, confirmation of choices, love, etc. Discuss the four considerations with your receiver before giving the exercise.

As you guide your receiver in this new method, the longest pause will be after the instructions for praying each word and before the invitation to end by saying the other four prayers in the usual way. After a generous time for the four prayers, conclude by giving your receiver time to converse with God. Show your receiver the words of the five ancient prayers printed after this first exercise.

Ignatius adds the following instructions: "If I find in one or two words rich matter for reflection, relish and consolation, I will have no anxiety to go further, even though the whole prayer time is spent on what has been found. When my prayer time is up, I will say the remainder of the Our Father in the usual way. And then the other prayers as named above" (*Spiritual Exercises* 254).

New Prayer Method 2: Breathing in the Soul of Christ

Preparation	I will allow the spirit to rest a little, considering where I am going and for what purpose. I make a gesture of reverence and humility. I read the prayer texts.
Opening Prayer	I ask for the grace to direct my whole self toward the Father.
Desire	I desire to breathe in the soul of Christ.
Prayer	I pray silently on each intake or expulsion of my breath, by saying one word of the Soul of Christ, so that only a single word is pronounced between one breath and the next. I do this with the natural rhythm of my normal breathing.
	Contemplatively, I pay special attention to the meaning of that word or to Jesus to whom I am praying. In this way I deepen my relationship with Jesus. I make myself ready for his action in me.
	I spend my whole prayer time on the Soul of Christ. When I am finished I say the Soul of Christ, Come, Holy Spirit, Our Father, Hail Mary, and Apostles' Creed aloud or silently, in the usual way.
Conversation	I ask Jesus for the virtues or graces for which I feel the greatest need.

Suggested Prayer Time: 15 minutes

Preparation: 3 minutes. Opening Prayer: 1 minute. Desire: 1 minute. Prayer: 10 minutes or as desired. Conversation: 1 minute. Listening Book after prayer: 10 minutes.

How to Give This Exercise

The title of this exercise is "Breathing in the Soul of Christ." It is day six, Tuesday of Week Two of this retreat. The content is the five traditional prayers but the method of prayer is different. The instructions for the exercise are straightforward, with similar pauses to last week. In practice, it is important for your receiver to keep his or her breathing normal, neither deeper nor shallower than usual.

The method is to have your receiver discover a rhythm in his or her breathing and word prayer, so that the exercise is both contemplative and focused. She or he may find it easier to pray a sense phrase on a breath or one word on several breaths. The focus is the meaning of the word or the divine person to whom your receiver is praying.

Ignatius adds, "If a complete prayer time has been spent on one or two words and I want to go back to the same prayer on another day, I will say those one or two words in the usual way, and then begin the contemplation on the word immediately following them" (*Spiritual Exercises* 255).

If helpful to your receiver, a nuance of this exercise is to simply "breathe in" the soul of Christ. Here your receiver could breathe the soul of Christ into herself or himself, or breathe inside the soul of Christ a part of his breath. Over time, either prayer is profoundly life-giving.

New Prayer Method 3: Progress through the gifts of the Spirit

Preparation	I will allow my spirit to rest a little and consider where I am going and for what purpose. I make a gesture of reverence and humility. I read the prayer texts.
Opening Prayer	I ask the Spirit for grace, help, and understanding of the gifts, that I may use them better for her greater service.
Desire	I desire spiritual progress through the gifts of the Spirit.
Prayer	1. I consider wisdom. What is the Spirit offering me here?
	2. Where is it present in my life?
	3. Where is it absent in my life?
	4. I reflect on the contrary of wisdom.
	After 3 minutes of consideration, I ask the Spirit for what I desire now.
	Our Father.
	The same procedure is repeated for each of the seven gifts.
Conversation	After going over all the gifts of the Spirit, I examine them as a whole. I ask myself:
	1. Which gift do I have in the greatest measure, more than any other?
	2. Which gift do I desire for greater service of God?
	3. Which gift would give me the greatest inner peace now?
	In conversation with the Spirit, I ask for grace and help. Then I choose one gift to live well today.

Gifts of the Spirit: Wisdom, Understanding, Counsel, Fortitude, Knowledge, Piety, Fear of the Lord

Fruits of the Spirit: Love, Joy, Peace, Patience, Kindness, Generosity, Gentleness

Suggested Prayer Time: 40 minutes

Preparation: 5 minutes. Opening Prayer: 1 minute. Desire: 1 minute. Prayer: 30 minutes. Conversation: 3 minutes or as needed. Listening Book after prayer: 10 minutes.

How to Give This Exercise

The title of this exercise is "Progress through the gifts of the Spirit." It is day seventeen, Monday of Week Four of this retreat. It uses the Prayer of Consideration. Your receiver may pray either the seven gifts of the Spirit or the seven fruits of the Spirit. The latter is better to teach your receiver this method.

There is a vast difference between knowing how to pray this exercise and doing it. To cite *The First Spiritual Exercises* book, "it is as great as the difference between knowing how to pan for gold on the one hand and doing it: desiring to find gold, searching for the right river, working hard to pan the gravel with the same repetitive motions, accepting days of no result, and feeling the utter delight of finding what I seek."

Four questions guide your receiver's consideration of each gift. As he or she pours their memories, experience and desires into each question, it is crucial to spend half a minute with each one in turn. The same should be done with the three questions in the fifth point of the exercise, Conversation.

The Particular Examen is made on the particular gift, sense, etc., chosen to practice each day.

EXERCISES COMMON TO ALL RETREATS

The Awareness Examen
The Particular Examen
The Reconciliation Examen
The Healing Examen
The Sunday Exercise
The Program for Life

The Awareness Examen

I give thanks	I give thanks for the graces, benefits and good things of my day.
I ask for help	I ask the Holy Spirit for help to discern my day with openness.
I review	I review my day, hour by hour, to see how God is working in my life.
I respond	I respond to what I felt or learnt in my review just made.
I resolve	I resolve with hope and the grace of God to amend my life tomorrow.
	Our Father.

Suggested Prayer Time: 15 minutes

Thanks: 3 minutes. Help: 1 minute. Review: 7 minutes. Respond: 2 minutes. Resolve: 2 minutes.

How to Give This Exercise

The best way to teach this exercise is to guide it first in prayer without any explanation. Then, after listening to your receiver's experience, take him or her through the directions for each point:

1. I review my day recalling its gifts, large and small, and allow gratitude to well up in me.

2. I make a prayer to the Spirit for discerning light in this examen.

3. I carefully search out how God is working in my life, moving hour by hour, through my day.

4. I respond. I might give thanks or express sorrow. I might feel delight with my Lord.

5. I consider the loving way forward. I will do my best and surrender the outcome to God.

From your own experience of praying the Awareness Examen explain each point with personal examples and the prayer texts. Spend more time on points one and three, and remind your receiver that focus is not on her or his life; rather, it is on God's life at work in her or his life.

Each examen has a similar five-point structure and dynamic but a clear difference in purpose. Your receiver may pray the Awareness or Particular Examens for weeks or months. The Reconciliation and Healing Examens are more likely to be prayed for a short time in preparation for forgiveness or healing. At an appropriate time, near the end of a retreat, you could go through different uses of the examens, encouraging your receiver to make them a part of his or her life.

The Particular Examen

Start of day

I resolve   Upon rising, I firmly resolve to carefully practice my particular desire today.

During the day

I mark   I mark each experience of my desire with a simple, symbolic action.

End of day

I ask for help   I ask God to help me see clearly in my review.

I review   I review the day to see how God has been working in my particular desire.

I compare   I compare hour by hour, day by day, week by week, my progress in my desire.

I resolve   I firmly resolve to act with my desire tomorrow. Our Father.

Suggested Prayer Time: 15 minutes

Desire: 1 minute. Review: 10 minutes. Compare: 2 minutes. Resolve: 2 minutes.

How to Give This Exercise

The Particular Examen focuses on a particular desire; as Ignatius puts it, "I ask for what I desire more earnestly in connection with particular things" (*Spiritual Exercises* 199). There is a good description of the Particular Examen in the *The First Spiritual Exercises* book, describing how the examen considers the "particular" in life. The description looks at dancing, seeking a doctor, using a road map, and so on.

The surprising conclusion is that "particular" is the way humans live at depth, the way your receiver searches with focus, heals, finds, enjoys, chooses, and acts, in union with others and Christ. All these shapes of particular are held in the Particular Examen.

There is a nuanced piece of advice for the Particular Examen. While your receiver strives to enact a particular desire, he or she could also ask God to act through it. Often God's action is the only way forward, even though your receiver is trying her or his very best. The Particular Examen walks with this tension of clear energetic purpose and surrender to what may be.

To progress more quickly, Ignatius suggests that your receiver makes a small, symbolic body gesture of gratitude when he or she receives the particular thing sought. This mirrors the "give thanks" step in the other examens. You and your receiver might talk about how this may be done briefly and discretely in a normal day.

The Reconciliation Examen

I give thanks

After reading the prayer texts, I stand for a few minutes before the Father, as son or daughter, and feel his compassion as he puts his arms around me.

I sift the month, with gratitude, for times I have received or given forgiveness.

I ask for help

I ask the Spirit to intercede for me with sighs too deep for words.

I review

I move through the last month, day by day:

1. Before the Father of mercies, I recall if I have rejected or withheld love.

2. In the light of the Lord's forgiveness, I sift my thoughts, words and actions.

3. With the Spirit, I examine the general direction of my life—my true self.

4. I explore one social structure I belong to, discerning good from the unjust.

5. I bring to Jesus any sin or sinful pattern that has real and deadly consequences in my life.

I respond

I enter the mystery of the Trinity's reconciling and forgiving love. I humbly express my sorrow for what was revealed above, and ask for forgiveness.

I resolve

I resolve to take one or more of the following paths to reconciliation:

1. To adjust my lifestyle or work, see a counselor or spiritual director, or deepen my personal, family and church relationships, so that the Lord may forgive and reconcile me through them.

2. To bring where I need forgiveness to Jesus, and call on his merciful love.

3. To take any needed reconciling action, for myself or others I have hurt.

4. To receive the Sacrament of Reconciliation, now and monthly if possible.

5. To make, as envoy for Christ, one small act of reconciliation next month.

Suggested Prayer Time: As needed

How to Give This Exercise

Givers of the FSE are often cautious about this examen. But if you swerve away from giving it, you may deprive your receiver of the very thing most desired.

Seeking forgiveness can feel like a journey into darkness or the unknown, but the God who meets your receiver must meet him or her in the worst of places, of memory and action, for only then can he or she really trust God's love. So give this examen with gentleness and kindness, but also with quiet confidence. Be assured that your receiver will seek reconciliation when and how he or she desires, at the depth she or he is ready for.

In the review and resolve points, have your receiver spend more time on those closest to her or his needs. The last step, one small act of reconciliation, is crucial. It reveals the purpose of reconciliation, ultimately an act to help others.

The Healing Examen

I give thanks	After reading the prayer texts, I stand before Jesus. He lays his hands on me. I sift the month with gratitude for times I have received or given healing.
I ask for help	I ask the Spirit to refresh, anoint and heal me.
I review	I move through the last month, day by day: 1. Where am I blind, deaf, dumb, or living a half life? Have I blinded or stolen the voice of another? 2. Where am I paralyzed by illness, a life situation, sinfulness, or fear? Have I paralyzed another? 3. Where am I tormented by demons, hurting myself? Have I demonized another? 4. Where am I dead, drained, grieving, or entombed? Have I taken life from another?
I respond	In God's healing love, I humbly express my particular need, as revealed above.
I resolve	I resolve to seek healing through one or more of the following paths: 1. To adjust my lifestyle, see a counselor or spiritual director, deepen my personal, family, and church relationships so that the Lord may heal me through them. 2. To bring my wounds to Jesus in prayer, that he may clean, heal, and give them new meaning. 3. To take any needed healing action, for myself, or others I have hurt. 4. To receive the sacrament of healing now and monthly if possible. 5. To make, working with the Spirit, one small act of healing next month.

Suggested Prayer Time: As needed

How to Give This Exercise

Ignatius wrote no Healing Examen, but he himself survived many near death experiences and suffered chronic illness all his life. The healing peace Ignatius received shone through him, and he specially identified with those enduring long suffering.

Perhaps more than the other examens in their placement, the Healing Examen is made very powerful by the exercises prayed before it. The Review points are potent because they focus your receiver's experience of each healing miracle, and special moments of a healing friendship.

In both the review and healing steps, direct your receiver to spend more time on those questions or actions closest to his or her need. The prayer texts include words from the Sacrament of the Anointing of the Sick and a text connecting healing with social action. These might be fruitful in conversation with your receiver.

The Healing Examen mirrors the Reconciliation Examen. You need to be aware that healing grace often appears as both forgiveness and healing, but they may be mixed or reversed or surface at later times in your receiver's retreat. The last step, like that in reconciliation, is for your receiver to take one small act of healing.

The Sunday Exercise

Desire	I desire to act in union with love.
Preparation	First I read the prayer texts about unifying love. Then I choose to seek that unity.
In the Eucharist	I focus on the doxology at the end of the Eucharistic prayer. Listening to this ancient prayer, I consider the way divine love flows through Jesus to the Father and the Spirit. And if through him, then also through me, with me and in me.
	After communion, I prayerfully watch all the different faces in the Body of Christ as each person walks past me to return to their seat. Through Jesus I am now a part of them and they are a part of me.
	I give thanks for the graces of this week and ask myself how I might express my union with him in action.
	or
In the World	I go to a town center, marketplace, or city square to pray. I sit there, at this gathering place or crossing place of many roads, and watch the flow of people coming into the center, remaining and then flowing out. Over this scene I imagine the Body of Christ and that all the people flow through him, with him, and in him. I imagine the love they receive doing so, how Jesus feels giving it, and how I feel to be centered in it.
	I give thanks for the graces of this week and ask myself how I might express my gratitude in action.

Suggested Prayer Time: As needed

How to Give This Exercise

Ignatius encourages your receiver to seek life in four special places. The first two are prayer and helping others. In them he or she comes face-to-face with God. The second two are Christian community and the world. Here your receiver finds God at work in all things, in all creation.

The four Sundays of each retreat have a dynamic that moves in three ways. The first way is that they flow into the sacrament of the Eucharist and out into your receiver's life. Thus renewed again in the Body of Christ, your receiver is ready to help others.

The second way is that they gather together the ideas of the particular movement of the week they conclude. They bring the personal relationship experienced in daily exercises into communal relationship with other Christians. The chosen prayer texts are pointed. The third way is that each Sunday exercise makes a four-part whole in the retreat.

The Sunday exercise is offered in two forms: through the Eucharist or in the world. So if your giver is a searcher, or responding to a mysterious inner desire, unchurched, or has been hurt by the Church, or if his or her circumstances prevent the possibility of going to Eucharist, he or she should be made to feel absolutely welcome in the Sunday exercise. It is to such people that Jesus went to first, in genuine friendship and deepest respect.

You can do no less with your receiver. Find a way to help him or her have the three movements described above so they too may knit the Sunday exercise into their retreat experience.

The Program for Life

Preparation	Immediately on waking up, I rouse myself to joy by imagining Jesus delighted with my Program for Life. I will get dressed with thoughts like these.
Opening Prayer	I ask the grace for to direct my whole self toward the Trinity.
Desire	I desire to create a Program for Life.
Prayer	I read the prayer texts. Then, I draw up an outline of a Program for Life:

1. What time can I take for enhancing family life? For children? For parents?

2. What time can I take for enhancing work life? For finding God at work in it?

3. What time can I take for enhancing personal life? Recreation? Exercise? Holiday?

4. What time can I take for prayer life? How often? Personal prayer? Communal prayer?

5. What time can I take for engagement in my church? When? For Eucharist?

6. What time can I take for engagement in my community? What service? When?

7. What time can I take for engagement in my faith life? For a retreat? For a little pilgrimage?

8. Is there a particular spiritual desire, awaiting action, that I have always felt?

9. Is there a particular work of Jesus that I desire to imitate?

10. Is there a particular opportunity I can use in the service of God?

Conclusion	After writing my Program for Life, I examine it as a whole.
	I consider my whole self and life in regard to it. Do they enliven each other?
	I end by explaining my Program for Life to Jesus, asking his help.
	Our Father.

Suggested Prayer Time: As needed

How to Give This Exercise

The FSE hopes, in the end, to have brought your receiver into the presence of the Lord who loves him or her so intimately, and gives so much, that your receiver asks to be sent into the world to give what he or she has received to others, even themselves.

A Program for Life will nurture this relationship and desire. It can gather and direct energies. It is a Program for Life for others as much as for your receiver, a program for one who is sent. Your receiver's Listening Book will help a great deal because the Spirit will have peppered past exercises with clues precisely for this exercise. A conversation with your receiver on the details of her or his Program will be of great help, as may be similar conversations by your receiver with her or his spouse and friends. Remind your receiver that the power to carry it out will be the strength of God working, not his or her own willpower.

Finally, Ignatius wants your receiver to set off in the right direction, like a pilgrim's ship he says, to set himself or herself at the arrival port of his or her pilgrimage—that is, in the supreme love of God. You might think of a way to do, or symbolize this, at the end of the retreat for your receiver.

THE GUIDE TO ENHANCE EXERCISES

"To find more readily what I want," Ignatius provides assistance below in the annotations, additions and notes of the Spiritual Exercises (*Spiritual Exercises* 1–20, 73–81). His text is used here directly or, divided for greater simplicity, written in simple paraphrase. This makes fifty notes.

Part one. The guides for enhancing prayer are best given at the end of the first week. They are self-explanatory. The next five guides, on enhancing the world of daily prayer, will require further explanation. Your own experience will help here. These guides may be given in the second week or when you judge them most useful.

Part two. These guides come from the annotations at the beginning of the Exercises. Annotations 6–16, in particular, are for the giver. The "best approach" guides can be given quite early in the retreat, even before it. The "during the exercise," "during the retreat," and "in general" sets of guides are given deeper into the retreat. The "during desolation" set is only given if your receiver is experiencing spiritual desolation. The "for the future" guides are for the end of the retreat.

In general, the best time to give a guide, or set of guides, is when your receiver experiences the truth of them for her or himself. With this cue from the Spirit, you can share the guides to strengthen, encourage, and clarify your receiver's experience. All this means you will need to become thoroughly familiar with the content and experience of both sets of guides.

Part One

To Enhance Prayer

1. Prepare the space.

   Creating a prayer space will keep me focused during the FSE. For my retreat, I make a small home altar with an image, flower, and cross. I may add symbols of light, water or desire as I experience a grace or need during my retreat (*Spiritual Exercises* 79, 130).

2. Think before sleep.

I take twenty seconds before sleep to recall the time I have to get up and for what purpose, going over the exercise I have to make (*Spiritual Exercises* 73).

3. Remember upon waking.

Before I allow my thoughts to wander, I bring to mind the subject of the exercise for the day. I then rouse my feelings by imagining the relationship I desire in it with the Lord. Thus I desire to know him more intimately so as to better serve and follow him (*Spiritual Exercises* 24, 74, 30, 131).

4. Consider while dressing.

Dress or dressing can be used as symbolic gestures of desire. So I imagine myself as I wish to be before the God of my spiritual exercise today. See the preparation steps in each exercise (*Spiritual Exercises* 74).

5. Rehearse beforehand.

When the time for my spiritual exercise is approaching, I will remember that I am going to enter the presence of God and then I run briefly over the spiritual exercise ahead of me (*Spiritual Exercises* 131).

6. Reverence to begin.

I stand at my prayer place for a minute, and with my mind raised up I consider how God our Lord is looking at me with tender love. In response, I make a genuflection or another gesture of reverence and humility (*Spiritual Exercises* 75, 131).

7. Body at rest.

For prayer I may kneel or sit, lie face down or face up, or stand. Ignatius adds that "two things should be noted: first, if I find what I want whilst kneeling, I will go no further, and similarly if prostrate, etc. Second, where I find what I want, I will settle down, without any anxiety to move on" (*Spiritual Exercises* 76).

8. Express generosity and desire.

    It is highly profitable for the receiver to begin with great generosity and freedom, and to offer all his or her powers of desire. This is in the preparation prayer and desire of each exercise (*Spiritual Exercises* 5).

9. Pray the exercise.

    Pray the full amount of time chosen beforehand (*Spiritual Exercises* 12,13).

10. Use the Listening Book after the exercise.

    After prayer, Ignatius instructs, "I will either sit down or walk around for a quarter of an hour while I see how things have gone for me during the prayer. The Listening Book, the FSE spiritual journal, helps with this process in depth (*Spiritual Exercises* 77).

To Enhance the World of Prayer

11. My physical world.

    I adapt the physical world to mirror the desire of the spiritual exercise. So I darken or lighten a room, I place a bowl of water, I wear certain colored clothes, and so on (*Spiritual Exercises* 79).

12. My emotional world.

    I remain in the emotional world of the spiritual exercise by keeping my whole day in serenity, joy, sorrow, etc., so matching the desired emotions of each particular exercise (*Spiritual Exercises* 80).

13. My inner world.

    I sustain the inner world of the spiritual exercise with thoughts and memories that keep the climate of my retreat throughout the day (*Spiritual Exercises* 78, 130).

14. My imaginative world.

    I enhance the imaginative world of the spiritual exercise by choosing what I look at, what I touch, what I smell, how I eat, where I am during the day. So I try to remain in harmony with the particular exercise of that day (*Spiritual Exercises* 81).

15. My symbolic world.

I use the power of the symbolic world by creating body actions that mark special graces or desires. The Sign of the Cross or a hand over my heart is traditional. Discretely, I may use similar gestures throughout the day (*Spiritual Exercises* 27).

Part Two

The Best Approach

16. Be at peace.

I need not be anxious about knowing enough of prayer, the Bible or church life to make an FSE retreat. I do not need to be churched. Nor do I need to be concerned about my past. None are necessary to meet God. My desire itself is more than enough (*Spiritual Exercises* 1, 2).

17. Value personal experience.

My own prayer will be more fruitful than anything I may read in a book or be taught by an expert. In making the FSE, I can be confident in my own graces and insights (*Spiritual Exercises* 2).

18. Seek inner relish.

Ignatius felt strongly that "the inner feeling and the relish of things" will fill and satisfy my soul much more than knowledge (*Spiritual Exercises* 2).

19. Practice reverence.

As my retreat advances, I will become aware of a growing intimacy in my relationship with each person in the Trinity. This will call for a deeper reverence in prayer (*Spiritual Exercises* 3).

20. Go with the dynamic of the four weeks.

The FSE takes four weeks. Each week opens a new theme, progressively guiding me forward. I will be happily guided, step by step, in each new exercise and prayer method (*Spiritual Exercises* 4).

21. Look for fruit in the right place.

I look for the fruit appropriate to the exercise I am making now. Everything else is a distraction (*Spiritual Exercises* 4).

22. Adjust the prayer time if needed.

I may adjust my exercises by making them a little longer or shorter, or by moving a day, if I need to. But I do not move them for ordinary convenience. Each retreat week has its own integrity (*Spiritual Exercises* 4).

23. Have a largeness of heart.

I begin every exercise with great generosity and a magnanimous spirit—as does my Creator (*Spiritual Exercises* 5).

24. Offer God everything.

I offer God all my desires and every freedom. I do so that he may avail himself of me and all that I possess. This offering is made in the preparation prayer of each exercise (*Spiritual Exercises* 5).

During Desolation

25. Be gentle.

In times of spiritual desolation, I will be kind and gentle to myself (*Spiritual Exercises* 7).

26. Ask for courage and strength.

In desolation, I ask the Spirit for courage and strength. I may also talk to the one giving me the Exercises, Spiritual Conversation Guide, spiritual director, or a prayerful, nonjudgmental friend (*Spiritual Exercises* 7).

27. Reveal the tricks of the enemy.

In times of desolation, I ask the Holy Spirit to lay bare the tricks of the enemy of human nature (*Spiritual Exercises* 7).

28. Trust the rhythm of consolation.

Spiritual consolation always follows desolation. Knowing this, I will take heart (*Spiritual Exercises* 7).

29. Discern the two spirits.

If I experience various agitations and thoughts brought about by different spirits, the good and the bad, I will seek out the Giver of my Exercises. If I am by myself, I may study the Ignatian Guide to the Discernment of Spirits in *The First Spiritual Exercises* book or use the steps outlined in the Spiritual Conversation Guide in this Manual. They will help me to identify where I am and how to move in the direction of the good spirit (*Spiritual Exercises* 8, 17).

30. Face suspicious obstacles.

If I experience temptations—when disheartening hardships, what people think of me, lost status, or fear of the unknown are suggested as obstacles to my spiritual progress—I should be suspicious. In a person moving from good to better, such confusion is likely the work of the bad spirit (*Spiritual Exercises* 9).

31. Expect resistance.

I need to be aware that the enemy will try anything to disrupt my retreat. In times of consolation it is easy to keep to my commitments, but in desolation it is difficult to last out. So, I might add a little to my usual commitment, so as to "get into the way not only of resisting the enemy, but even of defeating him completely" (*Spiritual Exercises* 12, 13).

32. Surrender to God.

In times of desolation, when I have done my best and sought the help of my giver of the FSE, I will surrender and leave everything else to God. I make ready for the consolation which is surely to come (*Spiritual Exercises* 7).

During the Exercise and the Conversation After

33. Focus on the present exercise.

I focus on what is sought in the exercise before me rather than reading ahead or considering any other exercises. Each exercise, day and week has its own particular order and dynamic. It is very important to stay in the place given in the exercise and not be drawn anywhere else (*Spiritual Exercises* 11).

34. Communicate directly with God.

As strongly stated by Ignatius, it is "much better that my Creator and Lord communicates directly with me, inflaming me in his love and praise, and disposing me toward the way in which I will be better able to serve him in the future" (*Spiritual Exercises* 15).

35. Know the role of the Spiritual Conversation Guide.

    A Spiritual Conversation Guide is not to sway or encourage me toward any choice or preference but to leave my Creator and Lord to deal directly with me (*Spiritual Exercises* 15).

36. Be open with the giver of the FSE.

    A faithful account of my prayer experience is useful not only for myself but also for the giver of my FSE. With my Listening Book, I ask: Where was I moved? What happened? Have I received what I desired? Detail here is very important. This is shared with my giver (*Spiritual Exercises* 17).

37. Apply the exercises to one's disposition and energies.

    I apply the timetable of the retreat to my disposition and temperament, making more or less exercises if helpful. Similarly, I may adapt them to my age and health, making an exercise a little shorter or in several parts over a number of days. Some days, I may have the energy to pray a little longer or repeat the exercise (*Spiritual Exercises* 18, 72, 129, 133, 209).

During the Retreat

38. Choose the right retreat.

    I choose the FSE retreat likely to give me the most help. I match my desires with the desires sought in a particular retreat. There is absolutely no profit to be gained from doing a retreat that does not meet my desires or disposition at the present time (*Spiritual Exercises* 18).

39. Reject unrealistic expectations.

    There is nothing in the FSE, either of content or process, that I cannot do. I do not need particular education, great intelligence, or perfect health. The FSE is for everyone. The only things I need are the generosity to take the practical steps of time and space and the courage to open myself to the God who loves me (*Spiritual Exercises* 18).

40. Be genuine and committed.

Making a retreat is not about being driven; it is more about surrender. While each retreat has four weeks of daily prayer and Sunday Eucharist, there is no deadline inherent in them. My life will have its own rhythms. I need to find the balance between making a real sacrifice and commitment and doing what is sustainable for these four special weeks of the year (*Spiritual Exercises* 18).

41. Complete all the steps.

The FSE has a deliberate order and progressive dynamic. I need to be faithful, to trust the order and leave out no steps—even if they seem obvious. Each exercise seeks not only to bring me to God but to have me do so habitually (*Spiritual Exercises* 18, 19, 20).

42. Know when to stop.

If a retreat is draining me and leaving me overly fatigued then I should stop—it is likely I am trying to make a retreat that is not suitable for me. I am a free, responsible adult; I can choose another time to make my retreat, or try a different retreat, or seek advice from a Spiritual Conversation Guide or spiritual director. Or I may choose to make a few exercises that really do attract and help. This may be all I need to do at this time (*Spiritual Exercises* 18).

In General

43. Let questions for information wait until later.

During the course of the FSE I may discover that I would like some particular information, instruction on the gospels, church teaching, history of spirituality, and so on. To follow this urge with immediate research or reading during my retreat will take me out of it and away from God. I will do better to note my questions and follow up on them after my retreat (*Spiritual Exercises* 18).

44. Let the examens guide you in the background.

There are four examens in the FSE: the Awareness, Particular, Reconciliation and Healing Examens. Each is introduced precisely, in rhythm and beat, with the exercises made that week. The Reconciliation and Healing Examens may be preparation for the Sacrament of Reconciliation and Sacrament of Anointing of the Sick, or similar ritual and action. The Awareness and Particular Examens embed my daily life into God's action in my world. After learning these examens, I can pray them, easily, and they will support me and all my exercises (*Spiritual Exercises* 18).

45. Let adult faith grow in the background.

It is useful to note here that the FSE does not have faith formation as a primary aim, but they do, quietly in the background, teach me most Christian beliefs and values (*Spiritual Exercises* 18).

46. Let the sacred word speak in the background.

With the solid scriptural foundation of each exercise, I will receive a very good overview of the Gospels and their content, as well as insight into Christian relationships, the active Trinity, and community from the rest of the scriptures (*Spiritual Exercises* 2, 4, 18).

47. Let the sacraments feed you in the background.

Each retreat has a Sunday Eucharist exercise. During my retreat, I will also be invited to receive the Sacraments of Reconciliation, Anointing of the Sick, and even Baptism. Alternative exercises are also suggested. Ignatius makes the sacraments an integral part of the FSE because he experienced God powerfully through the synergy of sacrament, prayer and Christian service. See the notes for the Sunday Exercise in this Manual (*Spiritual Exercises* 18).

For the Future

48. Take one realistic step forward.

The goal of the FSE is to take just one generous step in the right direction, not necessarily to make a major life change. Small, desired, slow, planned, confirmed, savored, realistic, free, habitual, fruitful steps are at the heart of these retreats. Only in this way can progress be found, maintained and kept. My Program for Life will help me to do this (*Spiritual Exercises* 18).

49. Be ready to accept great gifts from God.

Ignatius notes that our Creator and Lord desires us to approach and come nearer so that we can be "disposed to receive graces and gifts from his Divine and Supreme Goodness" (*Spiritual Exercises* 20).

50. Seek for inner peace.

The FSE hopes to bring me a certain peace of soul. This deep inner peace is a spiritual consolation and a gift of the Spirit. Over my retreat, the FSE may stretch me in my desires, take me into new territory, loosen that which binds, and place me, sometimes a little awkwardly, into new relationships with God. This interior growth and renewing change may unsettle me, but in the end God's inner peace will assuredly dwell in me (*Spiritual Exercises* 18).

The Returning Blessing

Bless my weary feet, Lord,
as I return from giving the First Spiritual Exercises.
Bless my mind with the knowledge of work well done.
Bless my mouth for the exercises received so well.
Fill me with gratitude.

Bless my ears to remember the treasures of spiritual conversation.
Bless my lips to share what I have learned.
Bless my heart to carry lightly what I have heard.
Fill me with lingering delight.

Bless my eyes for seeing how you live in my receiver.
Bless my soul for the reverence shown me.
Bless my body to enjoy the rhythms of grace revealed.
Fill me with happy consolation.

Bless my hands that carried your gifts to my receiver.
Bless my nose that pointed the way of the good spirit.
Bless my tongue to taste your goodness in this retreat.
Fill me with deep relaxation.

Bless my whole self, to receive your peace now.
You sent me out in love; now welcome me home.

ACKNOWLEDGMENTS

To those who have given the First Spiritual Exercises over the past six years, helping to test and develop them, thank you for the pioneering work. My special gratitude goes to Ruth Spierings, Margaret Fahey, Margaret Claver, Terry Fanning, Margaret Biviano, Frank Bourke, and the Campion Outreach Team who began it all, and still both give and train the FSE to great effect; to those who have been cogivers with me in the FSE retreats; to Bernie Miles who was there when we first discovered the power of these exercises; to Rachel McLoughlin and new givers chasing the Spirit; and to Michael Smith who first suggested that the FSE was the next big thing, and that I should write it up. The names of givers below are a short list. I am aware there are many others who have been quietly giving the FSE around Australia, New Zealand, and Southeast Asia; to you my thanks as well.

Marlene Beck
Angela Botti
Bill Brennan
Jacinta Bright
Bernadette Byrne
Angelo Campagna
Grace Chung
Trish Collier
Bernadette Collins
Larry Cox
Jean Cunningham
Steve Cunningham
Anne Dawson
Libby Delbridge
Gerry Ellis
Felicity Flynn
Mary Flynn

Cecilia Formby
Chris Gleason
Michael Gray
Clive Hamlin
Bob Hanley
Fran Hansen
Nicholas Hansen
Niloufer Harben
Catherine Hefferan
Kenneth Hezel
Ann Hoare
Kerry Holland
Kay Hooper
Joan Jennings
Kathleen Jones
Dale Keenan
Brendan Kelly

Elizabeth Ker

Maria King

Robin Koning

Mandy Lane

Ruth Morgan

Pat Mullins

Geraldine Naismith

Anne-Maree O'Beirne

Anne Priestly

Desmond Purcell

Moira Rayner

John Reilly

Jacinta Rice

Marea Richardson

Ken Robertson

David Ryan

Michael Ryan

Jennifer Sanders

Marty Scroope

Peter Shakovskoy

Maria Shelly

Jan Sobotta

Michael Stoney

Denise Sullivan

Frances Tilly

Peter Webb

Margaret Wiseman

Min Wullems

To my fellow Jesuits, coworkers, friends, teams of the Australian Centers of Ignatian Spirituality, whose support, work with the FSE, and conversations have enabled the FSE to come to term. Thank you.

Tom Lakesmith

John Doenau

Laurie Leonard

Campion Jesuit Community

Michael Smith

Ian Cribb

Patrick O'sullivan

Steve Curtin

Mark Raper

Trish Chisholm

Jan Geason

Peter Saunders

Robert Paterson

Marlene Marburg

Moira Rayner

Margaret Mary Flynn

Colleen Leonard

Jill Firth

Kathleen Walshe

Liza Stewert

Margaret Moore

Mercia Richards

Tim Molony

Dominic Tan

Pat and Vincent Lam

Peggy Goh

Niloufer Harben

Stephanie and Wayne Brabin

Deidre McInerney

Chris Gardiner

Bob and Pat Marsh

Orange Prayer Group

Sale Emmaus House

Maranatha Retreat House

Shalom House of Prayer

NOTES

1. This spread of the Exercises is detailed in J. O'Malley, *The First Jesuits*, 127–33.
2. General Congregation 24, Decree 20, 486–87; General Congregation 27, Decrees 221, 226, 572–73 in J. Padberg, M. O'Keefe, J. McCarthy, *For Matters of Greater Moment*.
3. General Congregation 35, Decree 2:27, 736–37 in *Jesuit Life and Mission Today*.
4. Edited by Joseph Tylenda, see http://woodstock.georgetown.edu/ignatius/letter8.htm.
5. Better Health Channel, www.betterhealth.vic.gov.au.
6. M. Palmer, S.J. J., Padberg, S.J., J. McCarthy, *Ignatius of Loyola: Letters and Instructions* (Institute of Jesuit Sources, St. Louis, 2006// Letter 11: Appendix 6, 674–76).
7. Quoted in W. Lambert, *Directions for Communication*, 16.
8. The Listening Center, www.sacredlistening.com.
9. Palmer, Letter 24: Appendix 1, 251–53.
10. Translation is by Joseph Tylenda, see www.woodstock.georgetown.edu. ignatius/letter8.htm
11. Palmer, Letter 24: Appendix 1, 251–53.
12. Palmer, Letter 18: Appendix 1, 239–47.
13. Palmer, Letter 24: Appendix 1, 251–53.
14. Palmer, Letter 18: Appendix 1, 239–47.

RECOMMENDED READING

For Spiritual Conversation

Bill, J. Brent. *Holy Silence: The Gift of Quaker Spirituality*. Brewster, MA: Paraclete Press, 2005.

Brady, Mark. *The Wisdom of Listening*. Boston: Wisdom Publications, 2003.

Byrne, Brendan. *The Hospitality of God: A Reading of Luke's Gospel*. Collegeville, MN: Liturgical Press, 2000.

Clancy, Thomas. *The Conversational Word of God*. St. Louis: Institute of Jesuit Sources, 1978.

Davis, Mark. *Breathing Spaces: Creating Spiritual Conversation in Groups*. Photography by Ged Barrow. Heswall, Australia: Rockpool Publishing, 2008.

———. *Walking on the Shore: A Way of Sharing Faith in Groups*. Chelmsford, UK: Mathew James Publishing, 2002.

Lambert, Willi. *Directions for Communication: Discoveries with Ignatius of Loyola*. Translated by Robert R. Barr, Marlies Parent, and Peter Heinegg. New York: Crossroad Publishing Company, 2000.

Lindahl, Kay. *The Sacred Art of Listening: Illustrated Meditations for the Heart*. Edited by Laguna Niguel, the Listening Center Workshop. Woodstock, VT: SkyLight Paths Publishing, 2000.

———. *Practicing the Sacred Art of Listening*. The Listening Center Workshop. Woodstock, VT: SkyLight Paths Publishing, 2003.

For the First Spiritual Exercises

Barry, William A. *A Friendship Like No Other: Experiencing God's Amazing Embrace*. Chicago: Loyola Press, 2008.

Keenan, James F. *Virtues for Ordinary Christians*. Kansas City, MO: Sheed and Ward, 1996.

O'Malley, William J. *Help My Unbelief*. Maryknoll, NY: Orbis Books, 2008.

O'Sullivan, Patrick. *God Knows How to Come Home: Reflections on an Active Spirituality for Today*. Melbourne: David Lovell Publishing, 1999.

O'Sullivan, Patrick. *Prayer and Relationships*. Melbourne: David Lovell
    Publishing, 2008.

———. *Sure Beats Selling Cardigans: Fostering Our Relationship with God*.
    Melbourne: David Lovell Publishing, 1995.

Silf, Margaret. *Inner Compass: An Invitation to Ignatian Spirituality*. Chicago:
    Jesuit Way, 1999.

For St. Ignatius of Loyola

Grogan, Brian, Idígoras Tellechea, and José Ignacio. *Alone and on Foot:
    Ignatius of Loyola*. Dublin: Veritas, 2008.

Ignatius of Loyola. *A Pilgrim's Journey: The Autobiography of Ignatius of
    Loyola*. Edited by Joseph N. Tylenda. San Francisco: Ignatius Press,
    2001.

O'Malley, John W. *The First Jesuits*. Cambridge, MA: Harvard University
    Press, 1993.

Ignatian Primary Sources Used in this Manual

The Constitutions of the Society of Jesus. Translated by G. Ganss, S.J. St. Louis:
    Institute of Jesuit Sources, 1970.

For Matters of Greater Moment: The First Thirty Jesuit General Congregations.
    J. Padberg, M. O'Keefe, J. McCarthy. St. Louis: Institute of Jesuit
    Sources, 1994.

Ignatius of Loyola: Letters and Instructions. Translated by M. Palmer, S.J., J.
    Padberg, S.J., and J. McCarthy. St. Louis: Institute of Jesuit Sources,
    2006.

*Jesuit Life and Mission Today: The Decrees and Accompanying Documents of
    the 31st–35th General Congregations of the Society of Jesus*. Edited by
    J. Padberg. St. Louis: Institute of Jesuit Sources, 2009.

*Personal Writings: Reminiscences, Spiritual Diary, Select Letters including the
    Text of the Spiritual Exercises*. Translated by J. Munitiz, S.J., and P.
    Endean, S.J. New York: Penguin Books, 1996. (The excerpts from
    the *Autobiography* have been reframed into the first person.)

The Spiritual Exercises of Saint Ignatius Loyola. Translated by Michael Ivens,
    S.J. Iñigo Texts Series 8. New Malden, England: Gracewing, 2004.

Michael Hansen, S.J., is a retreat leader, speaker, spiritual formation teacher, and spiritual director on the retreat team at Campion Centre of Ignatian Spirituality in Kew, a suburb of Melbourne, Australia. He also works in the post-ordination formation program for the Australian Jesuits. Hansen has served in several schools and parishes, produced radio and television programs, and is the author of five books, including *The First Spiritual Exercises, The Gospels for Prayer,* and *The Land of Walking Trees.* Hansen's academic background includes degrees in the arts and theology. He has developed creative uses of the Ignatian Spiritual Exercises and, with a large team of spiritual directors, has designed and given these exercises in many different retreat forms—both for groups and individuals. Hansen gives retreats around Australia and abroad, always seeking to make the tools and experience of the Spiritual Exercises accessible to as many as possible.

Founded in 1865, Ave Maria Press,
a ministry of the Congregation of
Holy Cross, is a Catholic publishing
company that serves the spiritual and
formative needs of the Church and its
schools, institutions, and ministers;
Christian individuals and families; and
others seeking spiritual nourishment.

———✦———

For a complete listing of titles from

Ave Maria Press

Sorin Books

Forest of Peace

Christian Classics

visit www.avemariapress.com

ave maria press® / Notre Dame, IN 46556
A Ministry of the United States Province of Holy Cross